I0517685

Praise for *The Seeker Within*

"*The Seeker Within* is a fresh roadmap for the new spiritual seeker and a personal guide for everyone who has questions along the way. Stacy has given us permission to use our voice, let go, and stay present in a busy world while building strength in our spirituality as it underpins your journey."

Emily Woods, Councilor and Reiki Master

"Reading this book felt like taking a walk through someone's real, unfiltered healing journey, with all the beauty, grief, uncertainty, and courage that comes with becoming more of who you truly are. There's no pretending here. Just truth, heart, and the kind of wisdom that's lived, not taught.

As someone who has also rebuilt her life from the inside out, I saw myself in so many of these pages. The way you weave nature, movement, nervous system healing, and intuition into your story is both grounding and inspiring. You aren't telling the reader how to heal, you're showing us what it looks like to choose yourself, again and again.

This isn't just a book, it's a companion for anyone walking through the fog and trying to find their way back to their own light."

Erin Gorrie, Bestselling Author, Speaker, and Founder

"It feels as though you've written my life experience. Different people, different places, but eerily similar lessons and discoveries. Somehow, you've done the impossible: charted a roadmap for inner growth that feels both deeply personal and universally resonant. Each chapter is signposted with the boundaries, resources, and insights that make the often messy journey of self-actualisation feel grounded and possible. I walked every step with you, from your climb in Sintra to your ascent of the Tor in Glastonbury, and shed a tear as you let go of what was no longer needed. What a gift this book is for anyone who's ever asked themselves, "Is this all there is?""

Genna Nelson, Naturopathic Nutritional Therapist & Health Coach and Trauma Informed Practitioner

"*The Seeker Within* is an honest sharing of reflections, offering transparency with no sugar coating. It was raw and real and connected me to more of myself through a lens of curiosity and understanding, providing beautiful examples to bring us into the experience and feel at a deeper level. It's not all pretty but it's worth it."

Carrie Scollon, Owner of FoundHer & Coordinator of the FoundHer Book Series

THE
SEEKER WITHIN

STACY KENNEY

R.P.P., P.T.P.

Soul Spark Publishing™
An imprint of Soul Spark Enterprises
soulsparkpublishing.com

Copyright © 2025 by Stacy Kenney
All rights reserved.

At Soul Spark Publishing we support copyright as a fundamental pillar of creativity, expression of diverse voices, exchange of experiences, and the creation of an expansive, vibrant culture. Thank you for buying an authorized version of this book and for complying with copyright laws by not reproducing or distributing in any form without written permission from the publisher or author. Your support allows Soul Spark Publishing™ to continue illuminating the world with words of wisdom, inspiration, and heartfelt guidance to all readers.

This is a work of nonfiction. Nevertheless, some names, identifying details, or characteristics of individuals have been changed. Additionally, certain people who have been listed are composites of a number of individuals and their experiences.

This publication is designed to provide accurate and authoritative information in regard to the subject matter covered. It is sold with the understanding that neither the author nor the publisher is engaged in rendering legal, investment, accounting, medical, or other professional services. While the publisher and author have used their best efforts in preparing this book, they make no representations or warranties with respect to the accuracy or completeness of the contents of this book and specifically disclaim any implied warranties of merchantability or fitness for a particular purpose. No warranty may be created or extended by sales representatives or written sales materials. The advice and strategies contained herein may not be suitable for your situation. You should consult with a professional when appropriate. Neither the publisher nor the author shall be liable for any loss of profit or any other commercial damages, including but not limited to special, incidental, consequential, personal, or other damages.

The Seeker Within, First edition 2025
ISBN 978-1-964445-16-8 (paperback) 978-1-964445-17-5 (ebook)

Book Cover and Interior Formatting and Styling by Lucie Ward
Graphic icon © MatandSterre on Adobe Stock

Editing by Michelle Ireland

THE
SEEKER WITHIN

Soul Spark
PUBLISHING

This book is dedicated to the seekers, the ones who are curious and those who wonder.

TABLE OF CONTENTS

PREFACE

Once in a while, as we go through life, a core memory is created. It is something that touches you so emotionally, so deeply that you can recall it in exacting detail. You remember the precise place where you were, what you were wearing, who you were with, what the weather was that day—even the smell of the room. A snapshot of all your senses is taken and it stays with you forever.

I have a core memory of a night that would ultimately turn into one that would shake and shape me into becoming who I am today. This particular night sent me down a path that I never saw coming.

It was Christmas 1999. I was in the communal living room of my Nanny's retirement home. The smell of turkey and overcooked starchy potatoes filled the air, with sweet notes of Earl Grey tea lingering. The laughter, the festive music, the excited chatter and gossiping were all flowing around our big family dinner table. I can even still see my Nanny in the kitchen with her apron on and curly grey/white hair as she tidied and served out coffee and desserts to her grown children and many young grandchildren.

The night was winding down. We were all getting ready to say our goodbyes, pack up, and head home to sink into a turkey coma after celebrating another holiday together. While I was waiting for the adults to finally leave, I started slowly exploring the room we were in. It was a common room that we hadn't spent a lot of time in before so I took the opportunity to look around on my own. A large black bookshelf on the north wall in the room caught my attention. I had always been more of a wild outdoor country child. You would typically find me running through the woods and digging up worms, rather than sitting indoors reading, watching TV, or even playing with toys. When I was outside, I felt as free as a bird.

I was always someone whose teachers would say, "Stacy forgets why she comes to school." My curiosity as a child sometimes caused me to become easily distracted. But at this moment, in front of a wall of books,

I was captivated.

My family was behind me, everyone laughing, carrying on, and teasing each other. My uncles were giving my cousins a hard time—verging on a full brawl, as was normally the case when they all got together. The women were gathered around the table "clucking like hens," as my grandpa Cecil used to say. As this was all happening behind me, I was quietly browsing the shelves and picking up random books. Then one specific book made me pause. I cocked my head to the left so I could read the title properly. There was something interesting about the title, something I had never heard before. *Soul's Perfection* by an author named Sylvia Browne. I had certainly never heard of her before, and I most certainly had never heard the word "soul." Like tuning an antenna to find a radio station, my curiosity homed in on this book. There was not a single thing inside me that could have stopped me reaching for it. It was instantaneous, like an impulsive reflex when you move to catch something that is thrown your way. I grabbed the book and immediately started reading through the introduction.

It was saying things like "the Other Side," "seeking," "spiritual growth," "resonated in my soul," and "journey of the soul." This was the first time I had ever learned that deep within a human being something greater existed. Something that was in direct connection to God or source of all life, spirit guides, a Higher Self, and a deeper sense of purposeful love and light for the world. I tuned everything out around me. I was no longer in a room surrounded by family, and the holiday yule and hustle. The sounds of screaming cousins and laughing uncles had completely disappeared. It was so quiet in my bubble that Santa himself could have come down the chimney and I wouldn't even have known. I was absorbed in my own world, completely dialed into this book, fascinated by each word on the page.

I quickly read and skimmed through the pages becoming fascinated about something more than my physical human body. As an active child, often outdoors running, skipping, jumping and swimming, I was very aware of my body. But this, this was something beyond that. It stated that I was connected to something much greater than what I could see when

I looked in the mirror. This book was telling me that there was a deeper source within—a soul.

This source within, our soul, apparently existed within humans, giving us life, and also had its own desire to learn and experience the world. It said that my soul existed within me before I was born, would be in my body for my entire life, and would continue to exist even after I died. Whoa! Mind blown.

Anything I knew about God only happened in the conversations at my childhood church and those conversations felt like God was a concept, something separate from me. The idea that an old man in the sky was looking down at me, either shaking his finger in disappointment or nodding in approval, never sat right. God was this far away, external idea and not one that I felt particularly connected to on the inside. Alternatively, *Soul's Perfection* felt very different—a deep connection to something much greater within myself and my life. I was holding my breath, I had chills over my entire body, and it felt like I had just learned a secret. It felt like I had just been initiated to a club I never even knew existed. This was THE moment. As a child I didn't know what all this meant, but I knew that something was different within me now that I knew.

I knew that I wasn't done with this book, so as everyone was finally leaving, I decided it was coming home with me—vowing to return it later. As I sit here at my office desk in Prescott, ON, looking out the window at the St. Lawrence River, I smile warmly looking to my left and see the book that's been with me since that very day.

I've kept it nearby me all these years to remind me of where my life-changing, spiritual journey began. It's been a book that shaped the relationship that I have with myself, and others, and reminds me to hold the bigger picture of life in perspective when I'm feeling lost, distracted, or alone.

Coming across *Soul's Perfection* was a random encounter in my life, starting an unexpected journey that forever changed me. I hadn't known books could offer me such power and understanding. And perhaps, just maybe, I was the right age, at just the right time to be in awe of what this book was telling me. Every once in a while when I feel a little lost, wondering what's next, or becoming distracted by all the things in life, I look at that book and it helps bring my focus back and reminds me to keep moving forward. As a woman now in my late thirties, I can only thank that curious little girl for picking up a book and never putting it down.

My initial awe of that book was the catalyst for my spiritual journey. But I'll never forget the silence of the moment, and the decision to follow my curiosity and pick up a book without any clue what it was about. Since then, my life has been one filled with spiritual wisdom from teachers unknown, the learning and unlearning of lessons hard-earned, innocent missteps, and so many joyful experiences. Picking up that unassuming book was like an initiation into a spiritual realm of feeling, trusting, and reflection. At the ripe old age of eleven, I was certainly glad to have had an early start on what would be the journey of a lifetime.

INTRODUCTION

This book is a culmination of all that I have sought, all that I have learned, and all that I have grown into since first sinking into the pages of the *Soul's Perfection*. These are the teachings, practices, ideas, and the stories that have all stood tried and true for me and my spiritual journey for over two decades. *The Seeker Within* is the welcoming in of the Seeker that rests within all of us, lying in wait to work alongside us.

The Seeker essence is something that comes from within. It's never malignant in efforts or misaligned with your highest good. The Seeker is motivated by your soul's wishes for you. It wants to celebrate the brightest moments of your life, shine light on the most shadowed, darkest parts of you, and bring love along the way. The purpose of the Seeker is to show you the obstacles that hinder you from your highest potential, and illuminate the next step for you. It's also there to remind you of the greatness that has always existed within you that you may have forgotten. Until now.

This book has been a lifetime in the making and my intention is that these words will act as a guide to anyone beginning the journey of navigating the path of their own spirituality. Your soul is unique to you, so life will offer lessons and opportunities designed only for you. This book is here to help you connect to your own soul as you begin to understand more of who you are, and how you relate to the world around you.

This path you're on will surely ask for growth, reflection and a lot of introspection and feeling. As we go through each chapter it is my deepest hope that this book will guide you on the way, and provide you with practical, sage advice. And should you get lost or feel disconnected along the way, know that you can pick this book up at any time to help call you home to yourself, lighting your way on the path that's right, and in perfect divine time, for you.

To all the Seekers...let's begin.

Chapter One

RED BRICK FARMHOUSE

My shoes are left behind as I run on the grass, weaving through the stones and rubble mixed in, making my way to the trails behind my childhood home. It's a warm summer day as I wander along foraging berries—picking only the best ones straight off the bushes, the juices staining my little two year old hands. There was no worry in the world. No chores, nowhere to rush off to, and nowhere to be. I suppose that's the bliss of ignorance that some children get to experience before the real world responsibilities file in and calendars fill-up.

For a small time in my life I got to freely explore and play with abandon. I often look back with fondness to the childhood that I had. It was filled with exploration, curiosity, and play, and the inevitable learning and growing that comes with being a very observant child. People often think that children are oblivious to what is happening with the adults around them, but early childhood education teaches us that this is simply not true.

From infancy through adolescence children are constantly modeling their behaviors around that of their external world. Their senses are acutely aware of what's around them, their brains firing at full steam as it stretches and molds into its full form. I've always learnt from watching, and growing up on a hobby farm there's lots to see and do and learn from.

I would spend my days freely roaming our family property making my own trails through the tall grass and surrounding woodlands. I was in love with finding my own way, having the best of times without a plan or destination in mind, exploring. "Just take a stick with you," Dad would say. I still stand by this directive today. I likely chose one too big for me, but carrying the stick would give me the courage to imagine I could protect myself, even though the sudden rustling of a squirrel nearby would cause my heart to momentarily skip. I was a tough little cookie. I fully believed in myself and for a little kid that was all I needed. Nothing could stop me.

I was born in 1988, to two baby boomers from the 60's. Mom worked in an office twenty minutes from home and was home every day by 5:00 P.M. Dad worked shifts at the local starch plant, a staple in our little town. Dad also acted as our personal weatherman. He could tell rain was on the way by the smell of starch from the plant filling the air— the aroma becoming heady as the sky would darken.

My first childhood home was a very modest two bedroom rustic red brick farmhouse. It wasn't anything grand. It was quaint and cozy nestled in the countryside of Cardinal, Ontario whose population never exceeded twenty five hundred people. To this day it's called a bedroom town. Somewhere you sleep at night but leave for work and entertainment. The house sat surrounded by spruce, pine, and cedar trees. In the back there was a large barn that housed many different kinds of poultry, an abundance of chicks, and a pony named Brownie. My sister Miranda, who was two years older than me, had been given Brownie for a previous birthday but we both shared in the fun of having her there. We would go back to the barn in the mornings and chase our chicks around. There would be hundreds of them running around scattering the floor turning it a sea of yellow, their little heads creating the illusion of waves as they would run from my sister and I. At two years old, I must have seemed like a giant to them. A role in a play I undoubtedly performed with gusto.

Outside of the barn there was a little pen that would house our old pigs, Eenie, Meanie, Minie, Moe, and Toe. We had a metal swing set across from the pig pen where we could swing and stare out across the yard and daydream.

There was never any question in anyone's minds that I lived most of my hours outside each day. I was constantly showing my badge of honour with dirt up to my knees, stains on my clothes, and tousled hair. My mother would put me in a pretty white Sunday school dress but it didn't take long for it to become a pretty brown dress. As soon as we got home from church, I was outside playing and exploring in my Sunday best. I would run to the barn, hide in the bushes, play on the manure hill, running wild and free. Stacy one, white pantyhose zero.

My father loved our home. When my parents bought our home it came with just over fifty acres of property to the side and behind the barn. We then bought an additional fifty acres to add to the property. I remember my dad laughing and smiling as he walked us around on our dear pony Brownie, cracking jokes and always making us laugh. Dad would even be smiling as he cleaned the pig pen, if you could imagine. As the trees and animals grew all around me, I grew with them. I became one with nature, blending right in. I was constantly on the lookout for animals, listening to the birds call each other from tree to tree, and follow the hum of insects as they went about their day. In the summer months I'd scan the fields for fireflies at night to create my own nightlight in a mason jar. I could smell a cedar tree before I could see it, identify certain birds by their calls, and knew exactly where to go to spy on more timid animals.

As snow fell it would signal the beginning of a different kind of outdoor fun. We'd take regular runs into town for free public skating, we'd build snow forts on our property, and the most fun to be had by a child in the country... snowmobiling. We owned a small arctic cat sled that we would drive around in the open fields. The motorized snow machine provided the quickest transportation from one side of the field to the other, saving my little legs from disappearing into the snow. There was nothing fancy or sporty about it, but it was never short in its supply of fun. Full days would be enjoyed outside only heading home to thaw or change out wet clothing. Otherwise, it was full throttle, buzzing around all day long. Happiness looked like chapped lips and wind burns on our faces.

Further back in the dense tree coverage there was a small opening where a hunting camp stood. It was a basic black highway trailer that got you out of the weather and stored basic cooking tools. Hunters would gather here on our property during open seasons and to celebrate their success of the season. Fires were built and raged on through the day, with old dry cedar trees providing an entertaining crackling as they went up in flames. We'd sled around the fields, through pre-planned paths, and when we were older, paths of our own creations. We had the freedom to choose how we spent our days and those days of wild abandon became my most cherished childhood memories. To this day I find myself lost in daydreams of the camp. Some days it feels as though I can place my feet back on the ground, breathe in the smell of the forest and wood smoke in the air, and feel a cool breeze as it sweeps my hair and cheeks.

The hunting camp was constantly filled with members of the community. Folks joined us for sledding, hockey on the pond, with countless friends of my parents dressed in orange and camouflage ready to begin or end a hunting season. It was a gathering place. But as I got older, and the years clipped on, I felt that sense of community and togetherness less and less.

When I was around three years old our family began building a new home on a neighboring lot that we owned. Something bigger and brighter than the red brick farmhouse. It was a larger white brick bungalow side-split. I got my own room in this new house, but there was no longer a hobby farm, just a vegetable garden that my dad maintained with his little helper, me. We sold the red brick farmhouse to a new family. We no longer had our little chicks, our five little pigs went to the market, and our pony Brownie moved up the road to a neighbor's farm to live out her remaining days. Our new neighbors in the red brick farmhouse had horses of their own, and we would sneak them apples or carrots on occasion to help fill the void of losing Brownie and all our other animals.

I helped my dad plant tree seedlings around the property. With our hands in the dirt, and with each new pine, spruce, or douglas fir seedling, my dad would share his vision for our home. The trees were to grow and provide a living privacy fence hiding the house behind its needles. With each new hole dug he would talk about building his and mom's retirement home on another lot next door. We planted trees in the adjoining lot so they were tall and ready for when their retirement came. Each lot was going to show a progression of our homes through our life's milestones. This was the idea, and my dad and mom worked so hard to make it happen. Eventually, a pool and deck were slowly added to our newly built home, and again the community came together to help with its build and enjoyment. A larger hunting camp was erected two fields back. "Cedar Cover Camp" was officially up and running, and our property was once again filled with people. The wisdom shared by people at the camp was something I would grow to treasure.

We lived in this new home for just over eight years. While the trees still stand, undoubtedly grand in their stature, I do not see them anymore. Turns out, not all things go to plan. Even with the best of intentions and thought out visions for the future, not all things come to pass.

Over the years, the community that we had around our home and extended property dwindled. Classmates stopped coming. We lived well outside of town, and if I really wanted a treat from the local store I'd have to hop on my bike and cover the fifteen kilometers into town and back. It wasn't a quick walk to a friend's house, and perhaps life in the camp and in the country wasn't an experience everyone wanted. It also became very clear that other kids didn't have the experience of seeing the fresh results of the season out on display.

The dawn of the Internet began to create distance even more within our community and within the walls of my home. I grew up right along with the Internet with computers becoming more popular and accessible. People were outside less and inside more. I was able to see first hand how this disconnected and distracted people from each other. At home, my parents reminded me of the grain ships on the St. Lawrence River near where I lived—passing each other silently, day and night. It felt like they were in the same place, but never at the same time. My parents' work lives could also have been to blame for the changes within my home, but I felt it was something more. Was this a result of shift work, passing schedules, or simply not having time to spend together?

This is also when I started to feel that, as someone who lived outside of town, I was an outsider—and the older I got, the more isolated I felt. Friendships felt forced and I slowly started to feel that I just didn't fit in. I even noticed how different my sister and I had become. While she played with Barbies, collected porcelain dolls, and straight As at school, I preferred being outdoors, watching movies, and brought home the consistent C average. While people were constantly buying more, I felt like I had less and less and comparing myself to other families became a large factor in the way I felt about myself.

With the growing pressure of school, and the social awkwardness I felt daily, I could never wait to get home, although as months clicked on I'd stare out the bus window wondering what the night ahead would be like.

In time, growing tensions and turmoil with my family eventually boiled over. I could feel the pressure cooker that became my home. It felt like one innocent misstep was an unexpected explosive ready to go off. I became hyper aware of my surroundings and the emotional state that others were in. I became so attuned to everyone else's emotions so I wouldn't mistakenly create more intensity.

What was at first a shock to my senses—the arguments, begging, and endless heated conversations, eventually became a comfort in normalcy. If I heard the fighting at night I knew both my parents were home, and I chose to find comfort in that. Sometimes I would lie awake waiting for the roar of my dads ol' Chevy as it came down the road and turned onto our gravel driveway. If they were home—together—I could sleep. The peace I had experienced in my earlier more carefree days had begun to transform into a different kind of peacefulness. Now having my family home together, regardless of how tumultuous it was, became the most important thing to me, even if I couldn't make sense of or understand who they were becoming and why everything was changing.

Navigating this new dynamic in my home caused me to become acutely aware of everything that was happening around me. I started to pay close attention to my parents, their body language, and the way they behaved on their own and around each other. I think they were trying to hide what was going on from my sister and I, but I could see that something was very wrong.

If there was one thing I began to understand, it was that my father and my mother were no longer happy. My memories of her contentedly tending to her gardens and flower beds became overshadowed by new scenes. Her crying while breaking a loaf of bread apart for stuffing for a Thanksgiving meal. Telling us to play outside while she sat alone with her sadness. My father would disappear to the hunting camp by himself whenever he wasn't working, with no invitation extended to me. In the past it was the entire family spending time together out in the fields, walking trails, or hanging out in the hunting camp as dad tended to the larger things. This family dynamic was something else entirely. A fracturing. My parents spent time alone away from each other as much as possible, whereas I just wanted to be with them both—at the same time.

The carefree freedom of years past was now something I had to work for—it was no longer simply a part of my life. I had to seek it out and create it for myself. I was going through my own changes as a young girl, and whether it was the stress of the home, changing of nutrition, or just part of God's plan for me, at ten years old I started my menses. The earliest of any girl in my grade at school, and even before my older sister. Great, one more thing to add to the list of things changing in my life, making me feel like an outsider.

So many changes were happening all at one time within myself that I didn't understand, let alone everything else in my external world that I couldn't make sense of. My sister and I were fighting more often, and were interested in different things. In efforts to not argue or physically get into an altercation with my sister I'd head to the back fields—my happy place. The moments I spent in the forest became moments with myself. I had grown up on this land and it was always a source of comfort and peace for me. I was now old enough that I would just go on my own accord. I'd naturally find refuge back at the camp. "Bring a stick," I'd hear my dad say in the back of my mind—bittersweet words of wisdom now. I'd walk the many paths that were clear and well travelled now. I would head down to the pond and listen to the beavers slap their tails as they heard me coming. I'd find an empty duck blind sitting just off the edges of the water nestled amongst the cattails and tuck myself inside. It's a small space meant to camouflage amongst the surrounding nature so it felt comfortable and safe.

I'd sit.
Quietly.
Listening.
Breathing.
Being calm and still.

I didn't know what was going on with my family, but sitting there alone, silently with myself, surrounded by the nature I'd grown up in, gave me peace in not actually knowing what was happening with my parents or what would happen to our family. Even if there was an undercurrent of turmoil waiting for me back at the house, in these moments of solitude, none of that existed. I was following an inner pull to create space for myself—to find time to simply be, without the turmoil of everything happening at home and within my body. Perhaps this was why when I felt the pull to the bookshelf at my Nanny's retirement home, I knew to follow it.

Anyone looking at our family from the outside could have guessed that my parents were done trying to stay together. There was no going back. Something had broken. They were no longer loving toward each other. The time apart increased. Their unhappiness finally came to a head.

My dad's old Chevy arrived in the driveway less frequently. Instead of being relieved that he was home, I would tighten. My dad was no longer the externally strong yet internally soft man that I grew up with. Something hardened in him—something I'm not sure he was even aware of. I watched him, confused about what was happening, as our parents grew quieter with each other and with us. There were no more jokes, no more laughter. The news soon followed that he had met someone else, was moving out, and bought a place in town. The tipping point had been reached, and the elephant in the house had finally been addressed. We were all venturing into the unknown, and none of it was in my control.

When I had returned home from school one day a man was at the end of the driveway, driving a stake into the ground with a hammer. In a state of panic, I called Mom immediately. She had become the solitary owner of the home in the separation. "They weren't supposed to come today," she said, and I could hear the sincere disappointment in her voice as she let out a long sigh. It forced a conversation to be had that neither my mom nor my sister or I were ready to have. Turns out, upholding a two-income house on one income, raising two girls on her own, caring for two cats and a dog, and actively traversing a largely public separation had become too much. The house had to be sold. The careful and intentional vision for our future was going to belong to some other family.

It all happened so fast it's almost a blur. The red brick farmhouse next door was about to become a distant memory, and the hunting camp that had been there for me my whole life was officially gone. Like puffs of smoke, one after the other, moments and promises and dreams, just dissipated with the wind. How did we go from what felt like having everything, to all of it disappearing in a flash?

Slowly we packed what was left in the home. The three of us plus our pets moved during the summer to a new town in Prescott, ON. I started a new school for Grade 7, and my sister began high school. I'd lay in my bed each night in a room that didn't feel like mine, and question: How did this happen? How did we get here? What do we do now? And, perhaps most importantly: Where can I go? Before, I had been able to go to the camp if I needed some solitude or peace and quiet. That was gone now and I didn't know where to find that safety and solace when I needed it.

I didn't know where to turn. I had gotten so accustomed to having a large property to explore and dissolve into when I felt unsettled and in need of solace, but I couldn't do that now. I would have grabbed a stick, wandered the trails, tucked into the duck blind and been alone with myself and nature. At our new home in this new town, this was no longer an option for me. I didn't know how to replicate those moments of peace and quiet.

Living in town was so loud. There were always cars. Neighbors were so close we shared a yard with them. It felt like a train whistle from the nearby track would sound every five minutes. I used to have this large outdoor space to work out what I was feeling or to just have a break from it all. Now I felt like I was stuck in a fish bowl staring aimlessly at the world around me with nowhere to go and everyone looking at me from the outside. I went from feeling isolated in one school to being the new kid in another struggling to create a solid foundation or space to settle into.

It was loud in my head all the time and I didn't know what to do. I was constantly questioning so many things that happened in recent months. There were so many unanswered questions that my mind would never quiet down. If I had been a fish stuck in a bowl, I could have shattered it to pieces through the sheer tension and anger emanating from me. I was looking for something, anything, to help me feel calm like the hunting camp did. I would later learn that this was me needing to feel grounded when my world had turned upside down.

Then on that fateful night as we celebrated Christmas together at my Nanny's retirement home, I was given some grounding. I discovered the bookshelf that changed the course of my life. It became a night that would start my spiritual journey. It would satisfy the part of me that felt so much unrest in my life. When my life felt upside down, I would finally start to feel right side up when I read that book. Seeing the book's binding felt like something was reaching out to give me a helping hand. *You're not alone Stacy, start here.*

I do believe that it was divine timing that led me to the bookshelf where someone so lovingly donated a book that would be what I needed at the exact right moment. Sylvia Browne's, *Soul's Perfection*, brought me out of my head for a small moment in time, a break from all the noise, and it was as if I felt my feet again for the first time in a long time. I felt a familiar feeling of peace while I read it. In the coming years, when I would seek the solace of the hunting camp, I would instead reach for the pages of *Soul's Perfection*.

Chapter Two

THE SEEKER

Everyone has a space within them that offers guidance. It's the feeling that nudges you to turn left instead of right. It's what comes forward when you have to quickly assess someone's behaviour in public. It's that moment of introspection when you envision a different life for yourself. It speaks in the moments when you absentmindedly stare out of the window and wonder what else is available out there for you. It appears in the moments before you dismiss it as irrelevant, not possible. This space, this voice, this guidance, it tries to connect with us in those moments, but many of us ignore it or don't even notice it happening.

Over the last twenty-five years, I have bounced between the internal and external world, striving to find balance, meaning, and understanding between what was happening all around me and what I was experiencing on the inside. I wanted to build a strong inner connection so I could feel resilient and grounded—especially if my external world changed beyond my control again. Houses can be sold, a life uprooted, and the symbolic rug pulled so quickly that without something internal to hold you up, a fragile foundation is sure to crumble with ease. How can you stay standing when you feel as if the rug is being pulled from under you, if you don't have the internal tools to help you endure and move forward?

During my transition into my new school and amidst everything that was happening at home, I began to focus on how to hold myself up so I didn't crumble. While the red brick farmhouse, hunting camp, and all the glory from my childhood became distant memories, they also proved to be exactly what I needed as an internal starting place to begin navigating a spiritual life at a young age. The moments I would spend alone in the forest behind my home became the foundation of my meditation practice. It inspired the serene scenes and backdrops for my moments of relaxation. It offered me material to pull from when I was beginning to practice gratitude. I knew my childhood had a mix of all emotions, but I also recognized how fortunate I was to experience something rare. Having grown up in nature gave me something to be sincerely grateful for every day. My early years in nature laid a foundation for my spiritual journey, and I pulled from my memories and experiences to fuel my spiritual development.

While I wasn't showing the best grades in school, I felt I was absolutely crushing my self-taught spirituality and meditation lessons. The questions about life kept on coming. I was so curious about the behaviours of others, as well as myself. I was trying to get to know the kids at my new school and neighbourhood, and I didn't feel as if I fit in anywhere. My new school seemed overwhelmed with bullying, and I never understood it. I would wonder: do people really wake up and choose to be this way? Where does the motivation come from to want to hurt a person? Where were the teachers in this, and why aren't they stopping it?

I would wonder if anyone else noticed how people were acting. Was I the only one questioning what was happening around me? This was something I questioned often at this time in my life, but more fervently at school where I could see something happening with my peers that was a true mystery for me. I would see it consistently throughout the day, multiple people acting by someone else's directive without a challenge. Kids would bully someone in their class just because another in their group told them to do so. And it wasn't only the bullying that I started to notice. I'd see someone in my class struggling, and I would wonder what they were battling, either at home or in their own thoughts, and wonder if they knew that they didn't have to struggle, that there was another way. These thoughts about my peers made me feel even more isolated and different and propelled me deeper into my own fledgling spiritual understanding.

I started to turn my inquisitive thoughts about my peers and my circumstances back toward myself. How can I move from the quiet realization that something inside of me needs to transform to actually doing it? I went from discovering what was lying beneath the surface to fully changing my thoughts or behaviour. I'd notice when I'd start to feel insecure around schoolmates. I'd remind myself that any difference I felt between myself and them was something I liked about myself and didn't see as a fault. Connecting to my guidance within felt like the right thing for me to do and be focused on. I was reading constantly and I noticed a recurring term that would describe someone who was on a mission to learn about this connection within. Seeker.

The Seeker. I knew immediately that this was true for me. This name, this term, this idea—my Seeker within—was alert and active and running at full tilt. To the next book, movie, website, or audio clip I could find and devour. The Seeker inside of me wanted me to ask internal questions, wanted me to grow and expand, and it wanted me to show others what was possible for them on their own journey of discovery. The latter was simply a whisper of a feeling at the time, but it was one that grew the deeper I went on my own journey to understanding spirituality and the role it plays in my life. But first, my Seeker within, wanted me to turn my curiosity inward and from there, grow in confidence and alignment with my intuition.

The Seeker is the part of us that refuses to accept surface-level answers, the part that refuses to accept what is commonly accepted just because it's always been that way or what everyone else is doing. It urges us to look deeper, question everything, and pursue truth despite uncertainty. The Seeker within us, wants more for us. More connection, more alignment, more fulfillment. Fortunately for me, once I connected with my Seeker, it didn't have to persuade me too much to commit to understanding it. I rarely responded well to being told what to do if I didn't agree with it, and I would question and not conform if it didn't feel right. Much to the frustration of any authority figure I found myself in front of. If it didn't feel right, I would likely question or challenge it.

The Seeker within us poses the questions and encourages us to go look for the answers. It doesn't give us the answers or tell us which way to go. Remember, it's often a nudge. A "hmmm..." that comes from out of the blue. The Seeker is that quiet presence that suggests that perhaps something isn't what it seems.

I was curious about the BIG questions, even from a young age. What was the truth of life? What is the purpose of humanity? Where do some of us get terribly lost? I would devour book after book and follow author after author searching for concrete answers, consistently coaxed along by my Seeker.

I learned very quickly that not every author had similar thoughts on those big questions and a lot of theories and beliefs were in conflict with another. I came across some even claiming their version was the universal truth, which as you can imagine, made the hair on the back of my neck stand up in uneasiness. I knew that what was true for me was not necessarily true for everyone else, so I could not grasp that there was a universal truth on the topic of spirituality.

We've all heard the saying, "If your friend jumped off a bridge would you do it too?" I used to think of this when I would come across an author whose work didn't sit well with me. It would be a similar feeling I would get when I'd witness groups of people following someone claiming to be a guru and saviour. Through my reading I honed this feeling. A guttural, visceral reaction would happen within my body telling me that this person or their information was not true for me. My stomach would churn as a repelling force turned me away from the source making me feel physically nauseous.

I use the statement "not true for me" intentionally because I do believe that what is right for one may not be right for another. I've learnt this over time, and I've had to walk away from social circles, unsubscribe from online media channels, and never read an author's work again because of the way it made me feel. While I walked away and decided it was no longer for me, their work is still out there continuing to influence others, and I think that is great—for them. I decided right then and there that my spiritual journey would be influenced by what felt true for me. If the information I was reading or teaching didn't feel true for me, it didn't come along with me for the ride.

I would later come to learn this word called discernment. For me, discernment is the guttural feeling of being turned away from something, wondering if it felt true for me or not, the pausing and questioning of a statement or directive was where my relationship with discernment began. Practicing discernment allowed me to slow down and assess how I was feeling. I began to use discernment when I would come across something new, a new teacher or topic, for example. I'd take a look at their following and see who their main audience was. If I was looking for empowerment, I certainly didn't want to be in a large group of individuals actively living in a victim mentality and being encouraged to stay there for someone's financial gain. I'd exercise discernment when an online coach would slide into my DM's asking me to join their spiritual course promising results before they even asked me what I was working towards. It taught me that some things can be right for another, and simultaneously completely wrong for me.

With information overload courtesy of the Internet, television, and large book stores, practicing discernment became an undeniable tool in my quest for understanding spirituality. Without it, I would have been left following the influence of another at the wave of their hand, believing that their truth would somehow also be mine. I came to notice that my intuition would show up first, asking me to pause, and then discernment would pop in immediately after, guiding me to look more closely at who and what I was learning from.

The more I used discernment in my spirituality the more it seeped into everyday life. Someone new had just started at my workplace and I was taking some time to get to know her. I was close with the owner and my other coworkers, but my intuition made me feel the need to pay attention to how we all meshed together. I felt almost protective, which was an early indication to me that something was off.

As I got to know her I knew that I couldn't trust her and that she also had no loyalty to the business. She'd pretend to be kind to the owner, but as soon as the owner left, she would say horrible things about them. I noticed the two of them became close as the months carried on, my own relationship with the owner started to fizzle out. One afternoon around the holidays I was called into the office. I was put on blast for overly indulging in treats that were gifted to the staff. I thought it was strange because I too noticed the treats had quickly dwindled over the day. Was everyone being called into the office? Surely, that would be the fair thing. No, this new coworker had thrown me under the bus stating I took them all, and while that didn't bother me because I knew my truth, the lack of curiosity from my boss did. No questions, just blatant accusations. Fully committed to the lies from a disloyal coworker. I'll never forget the look on my bosses face, or the betrayal I felt within me. I felt no need to justify, deny, or even defend myself. I already had no trust or respect for my coworker, but ultimately I further lost respect for the owner, someone I had previously thought of as a friend. My discernment steered me away from trusting and putting loyalty into the wrong person, and further illuminated other cracks in relationships I had counted on. Who knew festive treats could reveal such fragile connections?

In the early days of my journey, however, I had no idea what discernment was. I was learning as I went along, taking on the next spiritual text or lesson that crossed my path without giving it too much thought. Over time I would expand to new authors, spiritual teachers, and weekend workshops learning a little more of what I liked, what was important to me, and what I wanted to continue to work on. Like when we come across anything new and exciting, we dive in head first without giving it too much thought. It isn't until we've learned more about it that we become selective with what more we want to learn and from whom we want to learn it. The key here is to move from blind absorption into practicing discernment.

In time and with practice I would tune into my intuition faster and learnt to trust it more fully when it came to my spiritual journey. There were, however, still areas of my life where discernment wasn't as strong and lessons would be learned through trial and error. When I would look back, I would often feel defeated because of this. I started to believe that maybe I just needed to learn things the hard way, that maybe that was just the way for me. It was as if there were times where I just couldn't discern between what was right for me and what wasn't and it was incredibly frustrating. It has taken many years of diligently paying attention to moments when the Seeker within would say "be alert here"—asking me to pay closer attention to the moment, for it to become second-nature for me. It may take years of practice to develop your own discernment, but doing so will help you for a lifetime.

It took me time to realize that I had been scared to follow my own discernment. If something didn't feel right my instinct was to remove myself from a situation, and sometimes that wasn't always possible, or I didn't feel safe to do so. I didn't want to make the room feel uncomfortable, upset anyone, or put myself in any perceived danger. Instead, I'd ignore discernment and sacrifice my well-being. This behaviour of ignoring my discernment—and behaving in a way that I believed would be acceptable to others—would begin to follow me like a shadow, as the years progressed.

I think back to college prep days. A checklist of career options was placed in front of me on prospective avenues I could explore. These checklists would be taken into consideration when it came to my final year and the courses I needed to choose. At sixteen I needed to decide my future. Not one of these career paths jumped out at me. I could hear my family's voices in my head: Choose government, it's safe and pays well. Choose X because you'll be able to buy a house. Unsurprisingly, I eventually decided on a government position, thinking it would be the best option even though my heart wasn't in it. What I really wanted was to travel and see the world.

There was not one single moment in the designed plan towards my government career path that felt exciting or like something I looked forward to. It was stressful, required a move and getting my own place. The hiring process changed on the fly, and ultimately it was a path that led me—years and thousands of dollars later—to a dead end. I didn't listen to my discernment, and went down a path that I wasn't fully invested in. The inevitable outcome was not a surprise, because it was never anything I truly wanted for myself. It's an example of me learning the hard way— something I've come to understand is bound to happen when you don't follow your own path.

As I got older the word authenticity was being thrown around a lot online. It took off like a wildfire and soon enough I was seeing it every-where. YouTube channels and social media profiles and posts were filled with influencers speaking about authenticity. To me, though, it appeared like their followers or subscribers were all wanting to be just like their teacher. They would repeat the words from teachings, but it didn't feel like it held meaning. Where was the authenticity?

I came across many people over the years who followed their favour-ite spiritual influencers with unwavering devotion or worship. It was as if they were turning into being a copycat or lookalike of their favourite guru or celebrity, speaking about authenticity as if it was this easy thing to find, or go to the store and buy with the swipe of a credit card. Sur-face-level "authenticity" can be easy if you copy someone else, and I had no desire to be a copy of anyone. My Seeker was having none of it.

The Seeker inside of us wants us to find our individual passions and talents. It wants us to listen to our own inspirations and inner guidance. The Seeker within wants us to embrace the uniqueness that only our soul can express.

I learned that authenticity meant my path would look different from others' paths, and that a different path, while sometimes challenging, led me to living my life in my way, even when it meant going against what everyone else was doing.

Yet even after all this time of learning and reading and bringing spirit-uality into my life, I still didn't know who I was. How can you be yourself when you don't really know who you are? How can you introduce your-self to others when you don't even know? I kept searching, trying new things, spending money on workshops and mentorships. I should have been saving for the down payment for my own home, but instead I was searching, seeking, needing to know... My Seeker would not rest.

I put my money into personal and spiritual development because I believed with every part of me that it was the most responsible thing I could do, and it seemed to be contradictory to what many around me felt was right. I couldn't wait for the next paycheque so I could clear another book from my cart, or cover that payment plan for a course I committed to. I was signing up for another course and deep into my own journey meanwhile I felt pressure from others to be starting a family. Again, I was still in the midst of trying to figure out who I was; I was certainly not at the point in my life where I could focus on raising children.

I grew up in a family that prioritized the checklist of life's traditional achievements. Get married. Buy a home. Followed quickly by having kids. Nowhere on that checklist was investing in personal development. I grew up with that checklist being #goals, but I knew that my spiritual journey wanted me to blaze my own path, one that would ultimately be a path others could follow.

The Seeker within me wanted to create something different than what the checklist proposed. I felt motivated to spend time focusing on developing a sense of self, practicing how to be more self aware, and regulating my emotions before I was responsible for someone else. All of this became a priority for me, so that if I ever had a family of my own, I could trust myself to provide a consistently stable home environment for them to thrive and feel safe. I saw myself as a wife who could anticipate the emotional needs of her husband while also effectively communicating hers, and to be a mom whose children never had to grow up too fast all because their mom never did. I never wanted myself or future family to fall victim to—or suffer from—the consequences of my emotional immaturity.

As I continued to follow the nudges and questions of my Seeker, I started spending a lot of time and effort trying to 'un'become someone. I'd spent years unknowingly conforming to what I thought I should be doing. It seemed as though the Seeker within was asking me to find my authentic expression by removing all the things I thought I was supposed to do or be. This helped me learn that society was dictating a lot of my own expression, especially as a young woman. I was living in a world where everyone was trying to be just like everyone else, or expected to follow specific predetermined paths, whereas authenticity was saying: no matter what, you must follow your own path. The contradiction was becoming a difficult one to navigate.

Early Childhood Education shows that as a fundamental need, children just want to belong. This applies to all of us, even well beyond childhood. We want to belong. Most believe that to belong you need to fit in, and to fit in, you need to represent a specific image or type. There are over seven billion people on the planet, and you belong just as you are. It's our uniqueness that allows us to contribute our gifts to the world, to learn, grow, and find meaning in our lives.

Later in life I'd joke with my mom, "If there had been an option in highschool during college prep week to become a Buddhist nun, I maybe would have selected that." She thought I was joking; I was actually being serious. I wasn't listening to my Seeker within yet. As we discover who we are, we discover who we are not. Layer by layer we get to remove the result of old choices and become a more true expression of ourselves.

Chapter Three

MASQUERADE

As the Seeker acts relentlessly to guide you to finding your soul's authentic expression, it becomes clear that the more genuinely authentic you become, the more pushback or resistance you feel from society. To conform is normal, it's expected, and it's predictable. We are, after all, accustomed to being part of a tribe, and going against the tribe is an instinctual fear. We spend our lives, in one way or another, doing our best to fit in.

Even knowing that, I began to wonder why there were only the occasional few who seemed able to push against society's mold and become some of the world's greatest creators and thinkers, while others stayed blended into the masses of society. What were these people doing that allowed them to move beyond the fear of following their own path, and what exactly was holding everyone else back?

I looked closer and saw that some people feel uncomfortable being around someone who knows exactly who they are and can stand resolute in their authenticity. I wondered what the root was. Was it fear—for themselves, the other person, or society as a whole? What if it was something different? By now I had been on my spiritual journey for some years and my curiosity was still going strong. I had seen that when people faced something they didn't want to see, the reaction was either to pull back or push against it. Was it because they were subconsciously afraid to be found out for who they really are? I saw pieces of this within myself so I questioned whether more people felt the same. What was clear to me was that authenticity had the power to cut through the facade of smoke and mirrors we hide behind. The facade was acting like a mask, ones, it seemed, most of us were wearing. Were we then all participants in a masquerade?

I would see the masquerade in entertainment fairly often. It was always something relating to drama—parties and the like. I hadn't thought much about it or how it could relate to real life until one day when I was working as an assistant in a childcare facility. I was drawing and colouring and cutting out masks for the children to wear, the most wonderful and highly sought after mask was Batman. There was a young boy who was fascinated with Batman. I made a simple prototype and the room went wild. Next I was hearing chants of "Can I have a Batman mask, can I have a Batman mask?" They were flying off the table as fast as my colleague and I could make them. The next thing the teachers and I knew, we had created Gotham City right there in the classroom.

That night I was reflecting on the day and smiling and laughing at how invested these kids were in their imaginative play. It hit me. Costumes, drama, imagination, play. One thing led to another and the connection of how wearing masks grants you permission to take on a role came to mind. It made complete sense. When I started looking I would see it every day, and not just in the children in our care. I would see adults wearing masks on a regular basis, and sometimes wearing multiple masks within minutes of each other, switching with ease between one role and the next.

Of course these were metaphorical masks, yet when I started paying attention I could see them appear on myself and others. Attending a masquerade allows people to put on a mask and costume and pretend to be anyone they want to be. For an evening there's mystery, excitement, and the element of surprise. Temptations waiting for you at the bar or with an encounter with a stranger. There's freedom to choose whatever mask you want that allows you to feel anyway you want, and be anyone you want. Yet it's fleeting. The party ends, lights come on, and it's time to go home to real life. But do we completely unmask when the masquerade is done?

People wear masks all the time. As humans we are constantly flipping between one mask or the other. With this group of friends it's this mask and at work it's another. With my best friend it's this mask and with my parents it's this one. With a person we are attracted to it's a mask showing what we think are our best traits. We even have masks when we're out in our community and sometimes even with ourselves. Our masks become such a deeply ingrained part of us that it can be difficult to recognise that we're wearing them.

In the Seeker's drive for us to be authentic it takes an active role in removing and completely discarding every single mask we own, leaving us raw and exposed to the world. One after another they are discovered and discarded, but sometimes not willingly or without resistance. It can be extremely difficult to let go of a way of being that we've adopted over time. Sometimes we wear a mask that helps us feel safe in a social group, with family, or in our careers. We may believe that taking off the mask means that we will no longer fit in, leaving us unable to blend in, or even left standing alone.

It took me some time to discern between what I felt was a mask and how I showed up in the world of responsibilities. Was I wearing one all the time, or was it how I had to show up in a "role" within my life? There was a difference. One was a role that I played within my life due to responsibilities and expectations, and the other was a mask I wore due to a desire to fit in, be accepted, or feel safe. One was clearly isolated to job expectations and relationships, and the other was about how to "pretend" to be something or someone in an effort to maintain a connection or be seen a certain way.

Roles arise in different forms. I had the role of aunt, sister, daughter, girlfriend, friend, coach, captain, assistant, or student. Within each role I found I was a little bit different. Each one came with a different expectation. Was I wearing masks within these roles or was I just doing what the role required of me? Was I meeting expectations or was I trying to fit myself into a mold? I was plagued with trying to figure it out.

These are the questions the Seeker within you wants you to ask yourself as you discover who you are and how you want to live your life in relation to the world around you. Now that you're aware of the masks that you are wearing you can get curious. Why am I like that with this person? Why can't I just be honest with them? Am I pretending in my life? Why? Ask yourself these questions as you go about your day, and then, listen for the answer. Your Seeker will be guiding you through this.

While masks don't always ask you to pick a character they absolutely activate emotions, like how the little boy at the daycare would feel fearless and heroic while wearing his mask. The same happens whenever we wear masks. I noticed when I got home from work at night I was wearing a happy mask. Pretending to be happy when in reality I wasn't. I was doing way too much trying to wear way too many masks all at the same time. The car ride home was spent decompressing and by the time I walked into the house I felt like I needed to maintain a bubbly demeanor and pleasantness all over again. Sometimes I was just tired and needing support, but I was always the emotional supporter, so I'd don that mask and place all my needs to the side. I'd look in the bathroom mirror and mutter to myself, wondering when my state of being would get to be a priority. I'd pretend to be one version of myself, fully taking on the "fake it till you make it" mentality, but I was living a lie and I knew it.

I realized I was doing this all to myself, and wondered how many people around me were also in a similar position. Were there others out there pretending to be something they weren't? Were there others out there who were pretending to be happy, but miserable or exhausted beneath it all? Were there other people out there wearing multiple masks in front of multiple people in their lives only finding solace when their eyes shut and they drifted off to sleep and the masks finally came off?

These questions continued to plague me and I started looking at people with a deeper curiosity. On the drive into work or on the way home from the pub after a night with friends, I would sit and wonder why I was a certain version of myself with one person, and another version of myself with someone else. Why was I a certain way with one friend, and then completely different from the other? It was as if each of them knew two different versions of me. Did either of them know who I really was? Did I?

Choosing to wear a specific mask comes with expectations. If you take it off around friends, there's the chance you'll be seen more clearly. But why does this scare us? For example, say you grow up in a family who's passionate about politics. Maybe they are intensely supportive of their preferred party. Throughout your life you may hear conversations about their disgust for the opposing parties, or for the people who follow them. Secretly, this may actually be you, but you wouldn't dare tell them that based on the way they've outrightly judged and slandered people who feel opposite of them. You wear the mask throughout your life, and agree with them on all the same topics. It's just easier right? Maybe you witnessed someone disagree with them at one point or another, and the result was an uncivil exchange of words and disrespectful actions over the dinner table, or a complete cut off of contact.

Friendships and families have been destroyed over differing political views, and an inability to actively listen and understand each other. For your emotional safety you keep your political opinions to yourself, and consequently hide part of who you are away from others. You sit in a room with your family without granting them access to your honest thoughts. Without sharing your true beliefs they don't get to know who you really are. When they assume they know who you're voting for you agree and don the political mask that you keep around. You wear it all the way to the polling station until the attendee gives you your form and pen, and you enter the privacy of your own station. The mask is then removed, and you cast your vote. In the safety and privacy of your voting station where no opinion or judgment has access, you get to accept and be yourself. The polling station is symbolic of boundaries for yourself. With strong boundaries around your values and emerging desire to live a meaningful and honest life, you get to drop the masks and be your authentic self. These are the types of situations where we wear our masks like armour until we find ourselves in safety and feel able to take them off. Having multiple masks for these reasons, and wearing them for a lifetime can be exhausting so we have to be cautious with how many we're wearing and why.

I've had the pleasure of meeting people in my life who I feel are leading the way in authenticity. They've built a soul led business, tour the world on speaking gigs helping others find freedom, and seem to take no pride in small talk or beating around the bush. If they only have a few minutes with you it's going to be impactful, that's why people pay them the big bucks.

Being around them is sobering, as if there's an energetic field around them dissolving you of all the masks in your possession. It's intimidating, it's vulnerable, and it feels like being exposed. Their ability to see right through your fears and masks became a skill after uncovering and removing their own. With my own coaches and mentors I knew that they wanted the truest expression from me, and I wanted to be my truest with them. The opposite would be living a life of lies, filling spaces with smoke and mirrors, or even cowardice. I wanted the real thing. I wanted a real life. My coaches and mentors would encourage and celebrate the setting down of each mask that I had carefully crafted through the years, and the commitment I made to never picking it up again. There was a mutual understanding and compassion that to lay down a mask was a difficult thing to do because some of them I had for decades. To remove them and let them go was scary. Eventually I had to ask myself what it was costing me to wear them, and who was I without them? The latter is a juicy question.

Being different versions of myself with many different people came at a cost. I didn't know who I was anymore. I can empathize with the energy it takes trying to be multiple people around those that we love. We burn ourselves out, overstretch ourselves, and apply so much pressure not just on our own souls but also those around us who truly love and care for us

When I started to unmask I was in a long term relationship. I had moved to Niagara Falls, ON and we had been together for close to two years at the time. We lived in our own bubble prior to the move, and now lived closer to his family and hometown so our bubble expanded. I started to notice how I was consistently masking myself when around others. Did I feel the need to mask to feel accepted by them or to attempt to control their perceptions of me? I didn't know at the time, but I saw the masking in my partner as well. I was watching the person I knew and loved be someone completely different when we were around others compared to when it was just the two of us. This new realization that masking was leading to different versions of us in our new world, created a fracturing in our relationship. The inconsistencies of who we were being, living authentically versus wearing masks, led to such confusion, fear, and anxiety within me. I began to wonder whether he was being honest with me, and whether I was being honest with him when it came to who we were.

My relationship became my inspiration to change, and I'll always be grateful for it. How could I want something for him if I was unable to be brave myself and take my own medicine? To be authentic is an act of bravery and self-acceptance, and it asks you to show up everyday and work for it, no matter what.

Everywhere we went it was one mask after the other. With ourselves there were certain ones, around neighbors another, extended family a different set, and a group of friends another one entirely. I was tired, and I couldn't do the exchanging of the masks on a whim anymore. It was exhausting once I started to see how many I was wearing and I no longer had the desire to do it. Once I became aware of it, I couldn't unsee it.

After that it became an internal wrestling of a mixture of shame and fear every time I noticed I was preparing to mask up again. I'd be heading to a dinner or a bonfire with friends and would notice in my gut, that deep visceral twist that I had come to learn was my intuition speaking loud and clear. The Seeker within was speaking, and I knew it was that part inside of me that wanted the best for me and my life. It wanted me to have friends I could trust, who liked me for me, and friends who cared for me like I cared for them. It wanted me to feel safe and free to talk about my interests without fear of judgement.

In the moment leading up to getting ready to leave the house I'd go back and forth with myself. The whiplash from deciding whether or not to go would sometimes be too much and I'd just give in. I didn't want to mask up, but I also didn't want to raise eyebrows, or come off as rude. I'd hide behind loyalty to my partner, and make the decision to go, all while feeling uneasy and queasy, when I'd rather just stay home in my own space without any masks. It felt scary to be myself around them. THIS was a big red flag trying to get my attention.

The Seeker within is compassionate and unconditionally loving. It is understanding and will be there for you regardless if you make the choice to wear the mask or not. It would remind me that it was my choice to go out with my friends, speak about my interests, take up space in the room, and believe in myself or not. As I began to unmask I would sometimes feel as if life was one big costume party that I didn't dress up for. It felt like I didn't fit in anywhere. As I laid down more of my own masks I'd see more masks on others, and while I didn't want to be a part of the masquerade, I knew that the masquerade was part of life. I'd make the effort to be more my authentic self, not a previous masked version of myself. I began to give myself freedom to be a part of the world around me by being exactly who I was, not changing myself to fit into a social situation. At first it was difficult. It often felt easier to revert back to wearing my masks whenever there was a sense of confusion or uneasiness from others around my changed behaviour, but acting inauthentic now made me feel sick to my stomach. So, I chose the harder path.

The Seeker would consistently remind me that it was ultimately my choice to pretend to be something I wasn't or pretend to feel a way that I didn't. At first taking ownership and being accountable felt like a sobering slap in the face because there was nobody to blame except me. It's like the scene in the movies where one friend would be overthinking and in hysterics, and the other friend would give them a loving slap across the face to snap them back into reality. Holding myself accountable felt uncomfortable, and having nobody else to blame took practice in getting used to. Like a reflex, I'd want to blame someone for why I would wear a mask, and in doing so was releasing any responsibility I had for my own actions, and that's just not the person I wanted to be. I value integrity, and I needed to hold myself accountable for choosing to wear a mask or not.

I laid down my masks one after the other. As a result, I saw less people, and eventually had less friends. When I stopped pretending, ties between people didn't actually exist. When I was pretending to be someone

I wasn't, we had things in common. But when I took off my masks and went out into the world as my true self, conversations and spending time together became a struggle.

With the distance from certain people I realized that spending less time with them was absolutely the best thing for me. Being able to be my authentic self more often felt like taking a deep breath for the first time in years. The feeling became addictive. I was starting to like this feeling of being unmasked. I no longer felt raw and uncomfortable being unmasked. Going out in the world without masking up felt so free and light and full of energy. So much so that I started to notice everywhere I didn't feel it.

I had come to see and finally accept that I was pretending in my relationship. I pretended I was okay with eight years of no commitment. I pretended I was okay watching my twenties slip through my fingers, and that it was okay and normal to constantly rely on ABBA and the Mamma Mia soundtrack to set my mind straight until the next day. I pretended that I was okay with relying on drugs and alcohol to just sleep every night. I was pretending I was happy, and that we were making each other happy.

I was pretending that this relationship was it for me—the end all and be all. End game. Until one night I laid down for the very last time the mask I'd been wearing for years. The Seeker within was telling me that it didn't matter how many books I read on spirituality, relationships, or self-help—it wouldn't make HIM want to change. He has to want to do that for himself. My Seeker was also showing me that I was the one who changed.

That was a big realization, but not a shocker. Everyone has their own journey, and we were on different paths. After eight years, I was worn out, resentful, and I couldn't pretend anymore. I had a decision to make. Don another mask to prolong a difficult decision, or have courage and bring a cycle of pretending to an end?

I had to take a step back and look at my life from a bird's eye view. I had to look at the connections in my life and how they made me feel. I knew that in order to be authentic, I had to practice authenticity in all relationships, not just picking and choosing which ones. I encourage you to look at your life from an observer's view. What masks are you wearing and how many roles are you playing? Who are the people you feel you need to mask around, and pretend to be someone you aren't?

Becoming aware of the mask is the first step to rediscovering who exists beneath them all, and with new awareness, change can take place. The Seeker within beacons us forward to be our own unique expression. As you become more comfortable and familiar with your unique expression with others, you may find them being drawn to the real you.

Unmasking and growing authenticity grants you the freedom to live a meaningful life, one overflowing with self-acceptance. Over time you'll learn what that life looks like to you. Keep alert to life that surrounds you because you never know where or when your next lesson will turn up, or who will help you learn it.

Chapter Four

TEACHERS

The Seeker within is eager for the masks to be removed because within your masks exists a lesson about why you were wearing them in the first place. Each mask you discover and set down can become a teachable moment. What I didn't understand at the time was that behind each mask and lesson was an unexpected shift in awareness. Each lesson turned into its own curriculum in becoming someone new. Each personal discovery offered me a choice: react or reflect. And every reflection introduced me to a teachable moment, or even a new teacher.

It would be easy for me to sit here and tell you all about my favourite spiritual teachers, and believe me that is coming. I first want to offer some insight into how a teacher may come into your life so you can recognize them when they show up. In the spiritual community you'll often hear "when a student is ready, the teacher will appear." When I first read this a lot of prior interactions I had with others started to make a lot of sense.

Of course you have your school teachers growing up. Some people are fortunate to have a teacher or coach that stands out in the crowd as someone who was largely influential in shaping their character. The summer I moved schools after my parents separated I ended up in the classroom of Mr. Pratt.

To spread a little Christmas magic into our lives my mother booked a trip to Disney World in Orlando for Christmas and New Year. We were going with my aunt and uncle and their kids. A much needed family getaway. My sister told her teachers and collected all the work she'd miss while away and brought it home so she wouldn't get behind. I approached Mr. Pratt about my own workload and his response: "Don't worry about homework, just have a great time, and you'll catch up when you get back." While this was a wonderful lesson in enjoyment and grace it was more a lesson in building trust. Looking back, Mr. Pratt wasn't just a teacher in my school, he was one of my first spiritual teachers. From that moment forward I trusted and respected him. We had a wonderful trip at Disney, even more so because I relaxed and enjoyed myself immensely while I looked on at my sister and cousins slaving away on their school work at night.

As we headed into the summer Mr. Pratt pulled me aside. He told me I had been chosen to be part of a group of students who were selected to attend a leadership camp for a week over the summer. It was dedicated to teaching leadership through sports. I was ecstatic. Summer came and I was being dropped off at my very first camp, the Ontario Educational Leadership Centre in Orillia, ON. A week was dedicated to learning every sport I could have imagined. We'd move from tennis to lacrosse, swimming to field hockey. I was surprised that one sport that I had never heard of ended up becoming my favourite of the week, cricket. The week never slowed down, it was constant, sunup to sundown. We'd have our sport activities and mixed in between we would spend time learning how to show up as a leader for yourself and a team and how to communicate effectively with others. It was exposure to skill sets that I had never experienced before and have felt the benefit of them since.

I have never forgotten that week. While there were a few people there from my school there were two hundred more from all over Canada who'd also been selected by their schools to attend. A week flew by and summer soon came to an end. I felt like I was a whole different person when I returned home. To this day I believe that a week away at camp in the summer is a game changer for any kid. Just look at Hal and Annie in *The Parent Trap*. While my summer transformation wasn't quite as drastic as that I do believe I came home with new confidence and a greater image of myself as a leader and athlete. I went on to captain many sports teams right into and through high school and found myself naturally assuming management positions and lead roles in various jobs within my life. From that week on, leadership became something that I saw with great significance in my life. Leadership helps others feel seen and it helps others see something in themselves. I'll be forever grateful for how Mr. Pratt saw something in me when I was desperately just trying to stay under the new-kid radar.

I'm grateful for how he saw a potential and nudged me towards it versus pressuring me to assume it was something I wanted or should be doing. Most importantly, he let me choose. Too often children and adults are forced into directions they don't want.

I continued to lead, even going back years later to that same camp to be a counsellor. I can see the camp crest and logo of OELC on a shirt or pair of pants a mile away. Most recently I saw a young man wearing sweatpants with this very crest. We were sharing a flight back from Lisbon, Portugal. Halfway around the world and I spotted something that connected us. It's a very big part of who I am, and I don't know who I would have become without it. I look back with gratitude that Mr. Pratt was not only the school teacher I was given during a difficult time in my life, but also a teacher in life. He taught me how trust and respect is built over time and he opened the doors to leadership for me. He also gave me freedom from comparison. He never taught my sister, and was the first teacher to not compare me to someone else. The release from that expectation felt like a weight off my shoulders. For perhaps the first time in my life I felt I was enough on my own. It was an intervention in my life. It changed the way I looked at myself and what I saw within me, and in an even deeper way, it helped lead me towards a greater purpose.

Though I'm no longer leading in sports, I've found myself called to be a leader in spirituality. When I meet others who feel life has let them down, or feel as if they are falling behind in their own life, I feel a call to action. Within me exists an undeniable mission to ensure that a place is set at the table for all who seek healing, fulfillment, and love.

August 29, 2015. I was living in the Niagara region of Ontario and had become part of a growing online spiritual community in the area. They told me to go online and see what happened. The main page of my social media feed was blowing up with news articles about the passing of a famous spiritual teacher. Headlines read, "Wayne Dyer deceased. Spiritual teacher dies with family by his side." Over and over headlines like this flooded my feed. I looked to my bookshelf—which had grown quite a bit since sneaking *Soul's Perfection* onto my shelf—and there was nothing. Not one book by Wayne Dyer. All of these people in my community were fans of his work, and I didn't have one book? I had to rectify this immediately because I was obviously missing something.

The day that Wayne Dyer died would be the day that he became a spiritual teacher for me. The respect for his work is echoed in many who read his teachings, and if you followed from book to book you'd notice the progression of his own spiritual journey, which in itself was fascinating to "watch" evolve. While his early days were all focused on psychology he started to change directions into spirituality. He wrote a book called *I Can See Clearly Now,* a shared story about his lack of relationship with his father, coming to terms with, and ultimate healing from, his dad's absence from his childhood.

Where he was once filled with hatred for this man, he leads you to what his final thoughts were while standing at his father's gravesite. He came to the understanding that his father taught him all the ways he didn't want to be in his life. He made it a point to be the best dad to his own kids, and understood that it required his own experience with his father to ignite this within him. Keep in mind that this was not an overnight revelation. It took him a long time being dedicated to his spiritual path to get to this point of acceptance and gratitude. It was the work of years of perseverance to find healing. In the end, as he stood at his father's gravesite, he was overwhelmed with a peace-filled moment of realization and forgiveness. His father was a teacher for him.

Wayne Dyer's experience with his father is a contrasting example of what a teacher could offer to you. Whereas Mr. Pratt taught me trust, respect, and unlocked something within me in a positive way, Wayne Dyer's father showed him through his absence and abandonment how Wayne wanted to be for himself and his children, and was ultimately a lesson in grace and forgiveness.

When I find myself emotionally triggered by someone, I often ask myself: What am I learning now? Not all teachers offer gentle guidance. Some show up in chaos, conflict, or pain. But if we pay attention, their lessons are often the ones that change us the most. The unexpected lessons sometimes have the most impact. Look at the areas in your life that appear to have the most challenges or friction. Teachers don't always come in "inspirational" packaging. They may be the ones who are the biggest thorn in your side, and in your dynamic there's a lesson for you.

The Seeker within you claps with enthusiasm every time you stop in moments of uncertainty and notice when you're meant to be learning something. When things feel like they are going sideways there are two questions that are beneficial to ask yourself: What am I supposed to be learning here? What's the lesson in this? It's easy to get emotionally hijacked when we get stuck in traffic, cut off, or someone steals the parking space. Is the teacher the driver aggressively sitting on your bumper offering you an opportunity to practice patience or self control? How about the boss who is more concerned with how they look to their own boss rather than those they're leading? I've had many bosses who have taught me what humility looks like, and it wasn't because they were a walking image of it.

There are many others like Dr. Wayne Dyer whose work I look up to. Dr. Gabor Matè is a Canadian physician specializing in stress and trauma. His book *When the Body Says No* is an eye opener for all who are taking on too much stress or avoiding processing unresolved trauma and how this ultimately shows up in our bodies and behaviour. Dr. Joe Dispenza teaches tirelessly about how changing your thoughts and energy can have a tremendous positive effect on your overall health. He teaches that the more positive and elevated your thoughts are then the more likely your body will respond with healthier cells and DNA, leading to a more vibrant and revitalized life.

Becoming Supernatural—one of my favourite books from Dr. Joe Dispenza about energy centers within the body and human potential—features the concept of the Future Self. In some instances it's a potential version of ourselves that beckons us towards something greater and fulfilling. I tapped into this over time on my own and originally called it my

"Higher Self." I see your higher self as the best version of yourself, and how your future self would look if you were living your best life.

I had created numerous vision boards over my life with the focus on who I wanted to become and what I wanted to create. I was travelling often, and exuded happiness and vitality as my natural state of being. I was in a loving, fulfilling relationship. It was a vision, a goal, and one that I loved to dream about, but it was not something I was living. I was energetically unaligned to the dreams I had for myself.

My emotional state was far from happy, and as I reflected on my life, I wondered why. I realized that there were many things happening in my life that were not contributing to living a happy life. If I wanted to build towards the vision of the future I had for myself, then I had to start making some changes. My Future or Higher Self was showing me where I was not aligned to a higher potential. In this case, the teacher that had shown up in my life was myself. Nobody knew me as deeply as I knew myself. Nobody knew my secrets, masks, insecurities, strengths, or long-held goals and dreams the way I did. Removing all of the external teachers and looking deeply at myself was the start of the internal transformation stage. What's ready to be left behind will come rushing to the surface—if you stop and look honestly at yourself first. Looking at the root of what needed to change was confronting and scary, but I knew that I could only change if I was courageous enough to set it in motion. Your higher or future self will show you what's available for you, but it's who you chose to be energetically and the choices you make that will set that potential in motion.

People will cross your path who you don't realize are there to teach you something. Most relationships and connections offer the perfect opportunity to notice within yourself the areas you'd like to work on, or the areas you feel good about. The friend that barely calls teaches you the importance of checking in on your friends or to value friendship. The parent who lays the guilt trip teaches you the importance of emotional intelligence and maturity. The waiter who laughs and smiles while working for ten hours straight teaches you to have fun at your job and enjoy what you do for a living. Teachers are all around you, you just need to tap into your Seeker and listen for the lesson.

As you step into new possibilities for yourself and grow spiritually, and in a way that's authentic to you, you'll start to notice all the areas in your life that are not a match. Each choice you make is either energetically bringing you forward toward your Future Self and full potential, or pulling you backwards to living in your past. A lot of us are stuck in our pasts, replaying stories, events, fears, and conditioned behaviours over and over again, sometimes within yourself, and sometimes projecting it all over the people around us.

As you listen to the Seeker within and raise your own level of self awareness you'll be given the opportunity to see moments in your life that reflect a lesson that leads to change. Awareness helps you see the areas within yourself that keep you living in fear or lack. This ultimately presents a door to freedom that you can choose to walk through or keep shut. Crossing the threshold of the doorway to freedom happens when we bravely lean into the discomfort that change will undoubtedly bring on a spiritual path.

When you catch yourself replaying part of a past cycle, you have an opportunity to bring yourself to the present moment. Do you keep saying yes when you want to say no? Do you keep putting your trust in people who have not taken the time to build it with you? Taking advantage of these opportunities to realign to your Future or Higher Self is how we challenge old neural pathways and limiting beliefs, and give ourselves the freedom to choose differently. The moments that the Seeker within nudges you to notice old patterns are moments that grant you the opportunity to heal past parts of your soul that have remained stuck and are ready to break free.

Be open to the idea that teachers come into your life in all shapes and sizes. Their names aren't always on bookshelves or leading a class. Sometimes, they're everyday people down the street, family members, or those in your most intimate relationships—as I would come to discover. Your greatest teacher may, in fact, be the very person looking back at you in the mirror. When the student is ready, the teacher appears, and in various ways. The Seeker within will show you what's next to learn, and all you need to do is notice when class is in session. The lessons don't always arrive at the most convenient of times. I challenge you not to ignore the call—and to trust that it is always for the best, even when the lesson is this: there may be groups of people who expect you to pull up a chair at their table—a chair you eventually choose to leave vacant.

Chapter Five

CIRCLES

As you unmask your frequency begins to change—like changing to a new station on the radio. As you unmask, your new frequency may not be one that the people around you are listening to and interested in. You very well may have to find people who are tuned into a similar station as you. When we begin to show up differently, even in small ways, the people around us will notice. Imagine a group of your friends all listening to country music and then you show up blasting indie rock now. People are going to notice. It is very obviously different. Different, but not wrong or bad. Just different.

Showing up playing indie rock may make you feel judged. It may feel unsafe to stand out in this way. You may fear ridicule or negative criticism. These responses and fears are natural. It triggers our inherent desire to belong. However, your journey of listening to your Seeker within and following a spiritual path will help you find the courage to discover what is authentically you and find the people who are also living life to your frequency.

Each new awareness you discover about yourself will alter the frequency that is you. If you find yourself caring what others think about you then you may be making more of an effort to blend in and hide your true self away. This would create a fuzzy distorted frequency that never feels quite right—for you and the people around you. Deciding to be authentic means being genuine and embracing the vulnerability of being seen for who you are. The intention of your actions matters, and if it's rooted in a genuine desire to embrace who you are—in all your strengths and weaknesses—then you can bet you're on track to authentic living. This is about being yourself, accepting yourself, and cultivating a life around you that encourages you to be so. To be authentic is to stand in unwavering self-acceptance and honor how life unfolds specifically for you. This is when your spiritual practices—which we will get to short-ly—help build the courage within you to be different from your friends, family, and society and to cherish those differences, not to see them as faults.

The process of removing your masks, changing old patterns and ways of being, and growing personally can feel like you're the odd one out. One moment you're walking around feeling like you fit in, and another day you feel completely out of place. This feeling of being outside the circle is a common fear for people who start on a spiritual path and want to dedicate their life to living authentically and with meaning. When a costume you've been wearing comes off it can feel quite alien, and just as a country music loving person tuning into indie or folk it would stop you in your tracks, stepping into your authentic self in today's world can make you feel just as exposed—and just as judged.

It is common at this stage of your journey to be overwhelmed with thoughts of: What will people think? What if I'm not wanted? What if we fall out? It can feel like all eyes are on you. But I'll let you in on a secret. You're seeing more of the ways that you've changed than anyone else is. You're still you. You're just more yourself than you've been before. And yes, this can feel raw and exposing at first, you've been wearing masks and costumes for years, but now you're putting yourself authentically out there. This is an opportunity to find the places and people where you fit in without having to be masked up. Dr. Peter A. Levine, a renowned American psychologist, medical biophysicist and author of *Waking the Tiger: Healing Trauma*—a book I recommend to many—defines em-powerment as acceptance of personal authority and deciding the direc-tion you want to place it. If you're beginning to stand in your truth, setting boundaries, and notice you're ruffling some feathers, you're prob-ably doing something right. Likely, if you've been people pleasing for long, setting boundaries can seem aggressive or confronting. With a low baseline to start please remember this: You are simply speaking to your needs. This is not aggression, this is normal, and also part of introducing your authentic self to the world.

Finding where you fit doesn't have to be drastic. You might already have a small friend circle that's been built on authenticity, trust, or having similar interests. You may find you go on this journey together, and you may just notice your friendships and connections grow deeper. You may learn to communicate better with them or see them in a deeper way spiritually and with deeper admiration and compassion. It may end up that your friendship or relationship strengthens by you taking this step in life.

Like you, I have developed relationships and connections during different periods of my life. Some were inspiring and dedicated to growth, and some were created out of a need to feel a sense of belonging. They were all created out of a fundamental human need at the time. Over time, some began to no longer be a safe space in my life, while others came bounding in with inspiring stories and dedication to spiritual growth.

As I began to get more comfortable going out in the world without wearing any masks and being more authentically myself, I saw the power of outside influences and who we spend our time with. Some places I would feel great being myself, whereas other places felt like shimmying into a wetsuit. I slowly developed the courage to remove myself from tables I no longer wanted to sit at, opening up space in my life to introduce myself to people who inspired me to be myself. I also began letting go of connections I had made when I was a previous version of myself, a version where my low self-esteem had me clinging to people who didn't value me. Letting go of those connections taught me to value and choose myself. Remember, there are teachers everywhere.

While some are fortunate to have people in their spiritual journey corners, not everyone is surrounded by people that lift them up, or healthy peer groups that encourage them to embrace enriching life opportunities. Some of us are born into families who decide a path for them, ultimately ignoring what makes them authentic. For those of us in that environment, it may take until adulthood before we start to discover what is authentic and true for ourselves. As we get older, we get to embrace the freedom and free will to build enriching connections for ourselves, and allow ourselves to play and try new things. We get to build our circles up with purpose and clarity letting our values and discernment lead the way. Start looking at how you interact with the people closest to you and ask yourself: Where am I not exercising my free will? Where am I letting others decide my fate?

The Seeker within will have you looking for meaningful connections and encourage you to grow in your self-awareness. Because of that, the change in your circles may end up being the hardest part of your spiritual journey. Our closest relationships are where we put in the most effort and the people we care about the most. Acknowledging that we may have to change those relationships or close them out can feel daunting and make you want to settle and stop at this point of your journey. However, I encourage you to persevere and believe in yourself.

The greatest relationship you will ever have will be the one with yourself. Your ability to believe in yourself and be your biggest support system is paramount. This is why your spiritual practices are so often inwardly focused. Developing a strong and loving relationship with yourself will help you withstand the changes that may occur in our other relationships. It will also help you know that you are worthy and deserving of having deep and enriching relationships in your life.

When I first moved to Niagara in 2012 I connected with a local spiritual community. Prior to my move I started to become interested in an energy practice called Reiki. It brought my attention into my personal energy and taught me to tap into my energy stores. Paying attention to this allowed me to notice when my energy would feel depleted, and discover what factors were contributing to that depletion. It was something that was recommended to me when I was struggling with meditation. I had consistently been going for Reiki sessions, and adopting the principles before I moved, and I didn't want to fall out of habit. I would notice old friends or male figures in my life being a main energy sucker, but found myself lacking the confidence to end the connections. With consistency in sessions and open dialogue with my provider, when I discovered that a connection needed to end, I no longer hesitated, doubted my choices, or feared speaking up—I would simply end things. Throughout my sessions, I felt emotionally stronger and more courageous in my decisions and actions, and I truly valued the quiet time for reflection. My circles were changing, and each time my awareness would change, I'd see something a little more clearly that was next on the list to work on. I didn't want to let go of this new momentum and sense of confidence.

A couple nights a month there was a Reiki share group that met up at a local practitioner's house. This created an opportunity for me to get out, meet more people like me, and expand spiritually. Which proved to be exactly what I needed, in addition to the benefits I felt from Reiki.

This Reiki share group filled a large gap in the journey for me. Before I moved to Niagara I never really explored much outside my beloved spiritual and self-help books and local Reiki practitioner or monthly spiritual coach. My day was basically work, gym, reading, spending time with my boyfriend, and going to bed. Like a hamster wheel, it was the same day in and day out.

But when you try new things you meet people who can lead you to a new adventure. A key ingredient for this is to be willing to get out of the house, or join a group. I knew when I moved to Niagara I was ready to get outside my comfort zone and off the hamster wheel. There is a lot to be learned and many experiences to be had while actually out in life engaging with other people. You will learn more about yourself through interactions with others than you will just home with your books or online courses.

My social circle was very small, so in a way I didn't have a lot to work through socially. At the time, the few interactions that I had existed at work or within family and extended friend groups. I used my lack of social circle as motivation to widen my circle and meet new people. I realized that it's in the interactions with new people where you find the areas within yourself that require some personal growth. Their outside perspective on your life can leave a lasting impact. They see you as you are right now. They don't have decades of history on you. You may find that their perspectives challenge or trigger you, but those are the very areas in your life that are being spotlighted for further growth.

It is not uncommon to use these new connections and relationships as a jumping off point for looking at the circles that have been around you for years. You may find that, like many others on a spiritual journey, that authenticity and increased self-awareness shows you what relationships and entire circles might need to be overhauled. Because we've gone out into the world wearing masks and dimming our authentic selves for so long, it is easy to have been influenced and surrounded by the wrong people. When we look critically at the people around us, we may find that some are emotionally taxing, toxic, or have simply run their course. Again, this can bring up long-held fears of being alone or ostracized, but reach out to the new people and circles in your life and spend more time developing the relationship with yourself to withstand these necessary changes.

I share all of that with a bit of cheeky hindsight because I didn't approach this stage of my spiritual journey this way. I viewed influencing others as a way to bring spirituality into their lives, believing deep down that everyone around me needed it. My competitive side came out. Not wanting to give up hope for others—or risk walking this path alone—it felt like a self-imposed mission to hang onto connections far past their expiration dates, because I thought that if anyone could do it, I could. I assumed that all the people in my life could all grow together. I believed I could "hold space" for them to grow and evolve spiritually, and be a role model for them.

Holding space could have a whole book written on its own, but for the quick context of this book I'll share some insight. As you grow in self-awareness you'll also grow to notice areas within others where they may be stuck or set in their ways. To hold space says: I see where you're at, this is a space where you can be vulnerable and real, I'm listening. It doesn't say: I'll allow myself to be mistreated, it's my job to absorb your behaviour, it's okay for you to manipulate me. That's an important distinction. Some people hold space so well that when you speak to them it has a healing effect. They are present, compassionate, supportive, and not quick to judge or fix. Holding space feels like creating a container where someone can feel, express, and feel truly seen.

Oh how naive past Stacy was. I came to the humbling understanding that none of that was going to happen in some of my circles. There was no holding space for some of the people in my life to grow with me. There were no engaging or deep conversations about what I was learning, even though I was eager for them to learn too. My idealism came to an abrupt end when I realized that when you see things—relationships, circles, circumstances—for what they are, do not try to justify, manipulate, or convince it to be something it isn't and never asked to be. All we can do is focus on being ourselves, and if they want to come along with you, and are enjoying the new frequency they are feeling, great. If not, then that is great too. Holding space also means accepting that people are learning in their own time, but it doesn't mean you stop or slow down.

I started to ask myself if these people I was clinging to were actually contributing to where I wanted to be. Why was I so attached to them? Was it fear of feeling alone or like an outsider? What would happen if I let go a little bit? What would happen if I let go completely? It became clear that one of the main reasons certain people were in my life was because I alone was keeping them there. But my masks were coming off now and I was starting to create new habits and ways of living. I felt this internal battle to keep connecting with people I normally would or completely let go of the responsibility to keep the connection alive. What happened was when I let go a little bit, we spoke a lot less. When we spoke a lot less, we stopped connecting altogether.

I noticed that I physically and emotionally felt better the more I let people move on without me in their lives or them in mine. I gave myself time to grieve them and spiritually replenish from the energy loss I had sustained in connection with them. Had I truly wanted to keep a connection in my life, then it would continue to be something I prioritized, otherwise, it was time to be brave and let it go. I got to be more selective, and in turn, the circles around me got smaller, but much more valuable to me. Their friendship and connection became a genuine support system and I could trust that they'd be there when I needed them. It was security in friendship that I'd wake up grateful for every day. These connections were enriching, heartful, and vulnerable. I looked forward to spending time with them. The loss of my superficial connections was certainly buffered by the value in my deeper connections. Expanding your connections with aligned people will help as your previous circles begin to change. These new connections will feel at once exhilarating and grounding.

As I unmasked and learned more about myself, there were fewer and fewer people in my life. For some, having fewer people in your life can be scary. Society throws around words like loner or anti-social creating the idea that there's something wrong with you if you don't have friends. For others, having fewer friends means they are close with folks they trust, rely on, and have mutual respect. Your perspective on the shifting of your social world is entirely up to you, so spend some time on this. Your circles will change as you continue to remove yourself from the masquerade and continue to learn and expand from the teachers that come into your life.

Deciding to live a spiritual life will likely bring with it disruption. Regardless of how your circles shift and change, keep building the relationship you have with yourself so that you have the courage and self-awareness to stay true to what is aligned with who you're becoming along your spiritual journey.

Chapter Six

EAT, SLEEP, JOURNAL

I can say without a shadow of a doubt that when I've felt the most uncertain or off-center that the cause is that I've likely fallen out of my spiritual practice. A spiritual practice is a series of daily habits and rituals that help nourish our bodies, act as a grounding resource through daily life, and provide support for recovery and rest. I have a blend of practices that work for me—and may inspire your own mix. Likely, you'll play mix-and-match as you begin to discover what helps keep you grounded through the ebbs and flows of your journey. I always try to keep it simple. The more complex the practice, the less likely I am to stay consistent. After a long day if I'm faced with too many steps to follow I simply don't begin. If I start simple with a five minute meditation it can naturally become ten minutes, or longer if I fall deeply into my meditation. It's always the starting that is the most important, then your body will guide the rest. This is why keeping it really simple has been best for me. In addition to a few minutes of meditation each day, I like to journal about my day, my mood, something funny that happened or the spiritual lessons I may be currently navigating, and do some gentle movements to help move my energy through my body.

I want to remind you that this is a personal spiritual practice. What works for me may not work for you, and vice versa. Revisiting and revising your spiritual practice will be ongoing, and in itself, will become a spiritual practice. Once you've started unmasking, releasing, and realigning, it's essential to root yourself in things that feel beneficial and grounding, so find what works for you, and then adjust as your needs change.

A spiritual practice is a ritual of events specific to you. Some use the movement and breathwork of yoga to anchor into their body while others may go on a morning walk to create some inner peace. Others may start their day with meditations, like me, whereas others like to have their cup of coffee and journal. It's something that you do daily that helps set the tone to the start and end of the day, keeps you intentional throughout the day, and also ensures you feel grounded as the day begins and comes to an end. It's there for you to help you hold perspective, care for your personal energy stores, and in some ways, help you track your progress and lessons learned.

Your spiritual journey and how you navigate it is ultimately your choice, so please choose what is the best fit for you at this place in your life. Your practice is your greatest tool that comes with you everywhere in life, so it's best to keep it aligned and powerful. It's also the thing that's going to help keep you energized, and help you navigate the spiritual journey as it unfolds for you over time.

As we grow and evolve on our spiritual journeys it can feel like the ground is slipping beneath us. We may begin to feel ungrounded, or on edge waiting for the next shoe to drop, and it can leave the body in states of stress. Energetically, this makes sense, because change is occurring in our lives, and sometimes happening so abruptly that it can feel like once you adjust to one change another happens right away. Since we naturally want to be in a state of comfort, all these changes can put stress on us emotionally, mentally, physically, and, of course, spiritually. Your spiritual practice will help you ride the waves of change as they come and go. As you find practices that help you through it all, focus on ones that will shore up any rocky foundations you may have noticed in your life.

I want you to look at yourself as if you're a blueprint to a house. There's intricate spaces, lots of rooms and angles. It's a custom home with limitless room for expansion. With each new change that occurs during our spiritual journey the blueprint changes. Adding on a beautiful conservatory may feel overwhelming, so you may resist change, preferring to keep operating from your old blueprint. But, expansion can be an exciting time because of the possibilities it ushers into your life, and your spiritual practice will not only help you surrender to the new addition, but ground yourself in the new blueprint. I want you to remember: no blueprint, no person, is the same. Comparing your blueprint to another blueprint is a distraction from your growth. The intricacies and specifications of your blueprint are made entirely for you and no one else's is like yours, or yours like theirs.

Notice that you take a late afternoon dip energetically and that's when you revert back to your former ways of being? Add a practice into your day that gives you a reset in the afternoon. Find that your mornings feel rushed and that when you bounce around in the morning to get out of the house your day seems to follow that theme? Find something really quick that gives you a moment to pause and breathe in the morning before moving on to all the things that need your attention before leaving the house. Feel exhausted at the end of the day and end up scrolling for hours? Find something that helps you keep that in check while also allowing you to relax before bed. Trying to force your way through all these changes without having practices to help you, will be exhausting and ultimately, futile.

There's this beautiful parable that I heard many times on my journey. It's the "The Wise and Foolish Builders" from the Bible. To paraphrase, the story compares one man who built his home on sand and when troubled weather comes it washes the home away, whereas another man builds his home on a rock and that home could not be shaken. In the early moments of our spiritual journey we may begin to notice that we've previously built ourselves up on the sand, and it can feel like we are sliding down a steep dune to reclaim and find some stability. Sometimes the old, sandy foundation needs to fall so we can rebuild with intention, meaning, and alignment—and then, not be shaken from our home.

Eat: Nourishment for Energetic & Emotional Stability

A spiritual practice is created to help nourish you in your spiritual journey, both literally and figuratively. I've noticed over my journey that when there are a lot of changes happening all at once, that my food choices become a decision of convenience. A quick piece of chocolate or some chips to give me that quick dopamine hit and help me get through those tough days. Eating foods that are easy to grab or foods that just make us happy aren't always the healthiest or most nourishing for our bodies, especially when so many other things are changing and evolving. We need the support of healthy foods when everything else feels like it's in upheaval.

I remember when I went to my first weekend retreat. It was a Full Moon retreat that was hosted in a forested area in Niagara Falls, ON. Every afternoon a beautiful spread of food was provided for us. It featured all the colours of the rainbow and was pure vibrancy manifested onto a plate. Similar spreads have been consistent at each retreat or weekend workshop I've attended. Nourishing foods make our cells happy, and when our cells are happy, then we absolutely feel more alive.

But don't wait for a weekend retreat to create a rainbow spread for yourself. Our cells are the building blocks of life, so it's important to fill them up with proper nourishment. It's been a personal goal that no matter how low in energy I'm feeling, mentally or emotionally, that I will work my way back to nourishing foods if I've fallen off the nourishment wagon.

Eating a variety of healthy foods, as often as possible, has become one of my spiritual practices. It helps me keep one foot in the door of well-being even if/when everything else feels a bit shaky. Remember, keep it simple. It's not a complete fridge overhaul, but an introduction of healthier options being available to grab. Frozen fruits keep well, and can be thawed or added to many different options. You can even use fruit to act as aromatherapy, calling your senses to be present, as you slowly peel the rind off an orange and smell its oils fill the air around you. Connect with the food that you're eating. Notice if it's filled with the thrum of life or feels flatlined in what it has to offer you.

My nourishment practice led me to being more creative in the kitchen. Each week I would challenge myself to make one new recipe. I was inspired by my coworker Maria, mi linda amiga, "my pretty friend" as we called each other. She made some of the most incredible meals that I had ever tasted, and every time I fell in love with a new meal, I'd keep the recipe and make it myself.

Setting aside time to cook naturally creates a creative space. You can put music on as you chop, be fluid in your movements when things set to boil, dance around while things simmer. And then the smells... cooking activates all our senses and what a wonderful way to enjoy nourishing our bodies.

My one-new-recipe-a-week became a binder full of recipes that I love. Each time I cook from it I'm reminded of my friendship with Maria and the meals we shared together and with others. The addition of new flavours, new recipes, and time spent in the kitchen can be a space that not only is nourishing for the body, but for the soul as well. The creative sparks, the movements, and activation of your senses are all moments along the spiritual journey that can breathe new energy into life. Think about the last time you had a home-cooked meal. After just one bite, your soul feels refreshed and cared for.

Sleep: Reset, Regulate & Restore

I often struggle with sleepless nights. To this day, some nights I have a hard time sleeping more than a few hours. My thoughts used to race about how things were changing so quickly, or how certain aspects of my life still needed to change but I was too scared or hesitant to make it happen. When uncertainty of the future comes in, and I find myself standing on the edge of the unknown, my sleep is the first thing to take a hit. There may be days when I don't sleep at all, and if there's one sure way to make yourself sick, it's to be exhausted. While there are some people in this world who can run on four hours of sleep, I am not one of them. I joke with people that I'm a Leo and a lion needs its sleep, and anything less than seven hours of good rest will immediately show up as a sore throat, twitchy eye muscles, or a really sassy mood.

All the healing, evolving, and reflecting that you'll be doing along your journey requires rest. Do what you can to make sure you're getting a good night's rest as regularly as possible. If you're like me and loss of sleep is the first sign that things are simmering below the surface, build restful things into your practice to help offset the lack of sleep you're getting. I've seen far too many emotions run high and harsh words said because someone was exhausted and not thinking clearly. I identify as more of a morning bird than a night owl, so getting to bed at a good time is imperative, especially if you're a scroller or need that extra time to just settle down and find a good spot. Set a boundary with yourself around screen time before bed. We give this rule to children to help them settle down before a night's sleep, yet we continue to scroll each evening, activating our senses and stimulating our minds. An hour or two before bed, start putting yourself into a rested state, like turning off big lights and replacing them with lamp light, so when you finally make it to the bedroom, you don't end up lying there waiting to relax and settle.

I'm a huge advocate for leaving your phone out of the bedroom at night if possible, placing it on airplane mode or do not disturb to avoid lights or sounds while in bed. The lights are enough to dysregulate your circadian rhythms and one flash is enough to wake your body up when it is just ready to settle down for the night. Take some time to notice the lights in your room on devices and cover them in some black electrical tape if you can't find a way to turn them off. Our brains will pick up on the smallest light in the darkest room and, poof, there goes a good night's sleep. The darker the room at night, the better your sleep will be. Also, if your phone is nearby, you're more likely to look at it if you stir in the night than to breathe and ease yourself back into sleep. And when you're tired during the day, consider a nap. Even just a moment to "rest your eyes" during the day can be the exact recharge you need. Your body needs recovery time, and if you're already on the verge of exhaustion you tiptoe close to a line of burning yourself out, and absolutely nothing good comes from living in that state of being.

Spring of 2024 I felt myself stressed to the max in my corporate leadership job. Every day felt like I was living in survival. Instead of working through my lunch, my lunch hours became sacred to me. I would find the quietest place to just lay back and find some silence in the day to help me bring my stress levels down. Over the years I have listened to Abraham Hicks and what they have to share when it comes to stress, anxieties, and how to get back into ease and allowance. They shared that finding yourself pulled off center with worry, fears, or forcing things into being, will bring you out of alignment with life, and sometimes one of the easiest ways to come back into alignment is to take a quick nap, quiet the mind, and reset. Sometimes when breathwork wouldn't do it, nor taking a walk at lunch, I would go and have a nap, look out the window, or close my eyes for as long as I could. There's nothing quite as recharging as laying in the warm sun to help break up the work day and reset.

I look at having a good rest as an opportunity to hit the reset button. It's a chance to learn how to calm the mind, and for some it can be a great step into meditation. To be able to sit quietly and have dominion over your thoughts is one of the most empowering things you can do. So often we attach ourselves to the intrusive thoughts that we have throughout the day, rather than letting them pass by. And when we're tired, these swirling thoughts are often the outdated, misaligned ones, or bring about recurring patterns that hinder our growth. Tired thoughts can derail our spiritual intentions. But taking the time to rest or meditate during the day helps us to witness our thoughts. To slow down, pay attention to what is going on in our minds, and re-centre ourselves. It takes practice to notice which thoughts are running, and relies on your ability to distinguish and dismiss thoughts as you see fit. Over time, as I sat quietly during my lunch hour and on my meditation mat at home, some of my greatest inspirations would come and if I hadn't made the space in my day, I'm not sure I would have noticed.

Journal: Reflect, Connect & Witness

When I'd find myself up in the middle of the night, unable to fall back asleep and relaxing into meditation was evading me, I would reach for my journal. I hadn't always written things down. As a self-described wild child who felt more at ease running in the woods and playing in the dirt, sitting calmly reading or writing wasn't something that came naturally to me. Journaling was something I started doing more consistently in 2017 when I started working with new coaches and journaling was a part of the commitment to the program.

I had meditated on and off for some time, but I didn't always write my feelings down or let my thoughts flow to the page, and to be honest, a journal didn't feel like a safe place. It felt vulnerable, one moment anyone could know my deepest thoughts without my consent. The thought of it felt invasive so instead I kept it all in. Once I started to write things down

I would notice how one word after another would just come. When I set a time limit and let go of "what" I was writing about, or even how my writing looked, the journaling happened with ease. Sometimes I'd write something about my day, sometimes I'd write about something that surprised me, and sometimes I would even just doodle.

The book from my Nanny's bookshelf that I'd taken ten years prior talked about the concept of spirit guides. It said that you came to this world with a team of spirits around you that love you unconditionally and never leave your side. From conception until the day your spirit leaves your body behind in this lifetime and to the next, they are here with you. I found comfort and truth in this. On the days I felt alone on my spiritual journey I'd remember that I never really was.

When I journal, I often connect to my team. Some people know what their team looks like, or what their names are. It's never been clear to me, but I also haven't needed it to believe in their existence. All I needed was to feel the compassion that I felt when I would connect to them, and what would be left on the pages after I journalled. I'd leave my journaling time feeling supported, or guided towards my next steps. This was where I communicated to them the most. Many spiritual leaders offer free meditations on platforms such as Insight Timer and YouTube to help you connect to your guides and support your journaling. These meditations are typically around fifteen minutes—more or less—as you choose, and are dedicated to deepening your connection with your spiritual team.

If the idea of spirit guides doesn't feel true for you, then please honour this. Your spiritual journey is yours alone and the Seeker within wants you to explore and listen to yourself and what feels right for you at this time. When I first read about the concept I was also unsure. It only took me a few experiences of connecting to them before I felt safe and full of love and compassion leading me to know that it was something that would work for me. I knew it couldn't hurt my process, only add to it. Their presence felt benevolent, and left me with a sense of peace and support. If it feels like a big step to believe in or connect to spirit guides, instead think of your most beloved friend or family member who's passed over, or even the image of an angel or your Higher or Future Self. If there's one thing the spiritual journey asks of you, it's to be open-minded. So I challenge you to consider the possibility of what—or who—you can tap into for support: spirit guides or otherwise.

Your spiritual journey will benefit when you build a practice that keeps you grounded and focused. For me, it felt best to be rested, nourished with plenty of water and good food, and to process life and challenging times in my journals. Because of that, I've been able to look back on past journal entries when I was struggling and remind myself of how far I've come.

Sometimes when you feel like giving up, remembering how far you've come is exactly the motivation you need to keep moving forward. We can become so focused on where we're going next that we've forgotten how much we've grown. Reflection on your growth serves as a reminder of your resilience and can serve as inspiration to keep moving forward.

As mentioned, I have found the most success in keeping my spiritual practice simple yet powerful. There are no rules, no set structure to follow when creating your spiritual practice. Focus on what helps keep you aligned with your intentions and feeling energized. I knew I needed to eat, and I knew I needed to sleep so I started there. Nourishing foods and plenty of sleep. Then, as a human traversing the spiritual journey, I learned I needed to reflect and regulate my emotions when they felt overwhelming and be present with the lessons I was learning, so journaling and meditation became part of my practice. Each part of my practice supported an important aspect of my life, or added value to another. Create a practice around behaviours that empower and better you when you feel distracted, overwhelmed, or just need a little bit of help.

When life can feel like it's changing all around you, having an anchor point really helps. Let your spiritual practice be that for you. Remember to keep it simple, and if all else fails: eat, sleep, journal.

Chapter Seven

BUCKLE UP AND BUCKLE DOWN

With greater awareness comes greater truth. I've heard, almost verbatim, something from many people over the last twenty years, about their experiences of their spiritual journey: *If I knew then what I know now, I'm not sure I would have started. Sometimes I wish I never went down this road.* It is important for me to share this with you because when I started on my spiritual journey I didn't fully understand how confronting or challenging it could be.

Spirituality as I experienced in the early days, felt or looked to be much more of a light-and-love culture devoid of any conflict or hardship. I'd see people on social media or who had been following a spiritual path for a long time and it seemed like they were always so positive. That was one of the aspects that drew me in. I wanted to be around positive people, but what I didn't see was the selective editing out of the hardship that can come along with a spiritual path.

This, to me, is a great disservice. If we can be better prepared for what may come then we can rise to the occasion and conquer the challenges versus fall to discouragement or avoidance. I understand that promoting the struggle may not get you the social media views and likes, but I have been known to connect on a deeper level to those who aren't afraid to share their toughest moments and vulnerabilities on their spiritual journey.

In 1980 a term "spiritual bypassing" began being used to describe someone who, rather than delve into their unresolved conflict, would hide behind light-and-love. It was a way for someone to avoid getting to the root of a problem or do the inner work to discover what was ready to transform. While the term was coined in 1980 I didn't learn this until well into the 2000's. I didn't realize I was even doing it until I came toe-to-toe with a hard truth about my life and a long term relationship I had been in. I could no longer run from it, and there was no tarot card, or positive affirmation that was going to change the internal conflict I had been experiencing.

Sometimes it's the admission of where things aren't working, the unmasking and acceptance of what is, where your spiritual journey can accelerate your growth. Growth happens when we admit to what binds our energy, and holds us back from true freedom and expression. Nothing will slow your journey down more than the avoidance or the refusal to confront the habits or people that are sucking the life force right out of you.

The spiritual journey is a one-step-at-a-time experience of discovery and opportunity to change. Some people make a shift into spirituality after being redirected by a breakdown in their life, and some shift to spirituality because they've found themselves seeking deeper meaning and purpose in life and want to know themselves better.

As we embrace the Seeker within we begin to notice the many facades that surround all aspects of our lives. As our masquerade masks fall, our circles can start to be tested. Friendships, relationships, and even workplace connections get the critical spotlight put on them. Your family dynamics may begin to take a different form. You're able to see with clearer eyes any deep dysfunction that you didn't know was there or weren't able to admit to, and even where some of your own dysfunctions got their origins.

One after the other it can seem like nothing around you makes sense. From the many conversations I've had over the years, this is where the original sentiment of, "sometimes I wish I never went down this road" was born. The spiritual journey can be a sensory and emotional overload and seems as if every time you turn around there's a new truth looking for a confession, or the noticing of a habit or trait that's become very hard to break no matter how hard you try. For some, this is the "dark night of the soul" phase. It's where everywhere you look things seem to be changing, and as you try to make sense of one thing, another falls apart or comes to light. It can feel discouraging and just downright painful and exhaustive.

My own dark night of the soul phase brought me into deep introspection. There were memories surfacing where repeated patterns I was in or decisions I had made over and over again filled the pages of my journals. It was emotionally overwhelming and brought with it waves of grief for life unlived or times I felt robbed of happiness. This was also when I, surprisingly, began to read and write poetry. It rose up organically and I made the point of writing things down as rhymes came into my head. My heart was starting to release repressed hurt and anger, and one day I noticed the journaling in my spiritual practice was rhythmic, vulnerable, and eloquent, feeling almost like a song. My creativity was flowing out of me the more I allowed myself to feel through past hurts. I'd sing. I'd write. I would find opportunities to paint, or pick up my violin from many years past. I'd dance and sway to the rhythm of songs and close my eyes while enjoying Spanish guitar. This dark night the soul part of the journey can be alchemized or transformed into some of the best creativity and art. If you feel this phase is coming, your creativity may be ready to shine or to discover the heartfelt work of an artist, new and old like my main man Rumi.

Though many of us have said we wouldn't have started had we known how difficult and confronting our spiritual journey would be, we were all still on the journey. We were still here, dedicated to our growth. We were not giving up. None of us were. There comes a point along the way when you look around and realize that everything is different now. There is no going back. And that realization can be overwhelming.

This is why it's important to have some type of community around you where you feel inspired by their authenticity and admire the work they've put into their growth. This crushing moment of realization can feel heavy when you're alone, and to be reminded that we've all been there, and that someone is there for you through this, can be a massive boost of confidence, or, at the very least, inspiring in the moment, and just what you need to keep moving forward.

The spiritual journey is one of the most intense, energetic, and emotional roller coasters that you'll ever ride and you'll queue up to do it over and over again. Each day you are granted opportunities to transform your life. From the moment you wake up until the moment you lay your head down to sleep, your day is filled with choices—in actions, beliefs, and thoughts. You'll start to recognize the moments when you choose out of ego, scarcity or fear—and in those same moments, you'll have the power to take a stand for your right to be here and live a fulfilling life, just like those who came before you. You matter, just as much as everyone else.

My stomach would twist and tighten when I finally noticed the obviousness of one of my traits that I had been keeping active even though it stopped being beneficial years prior. That sick feeling of noticing that I was perpetuating something that wasn't good for me. That shadow of feeling unimportant and not enough, rooted in my childhood, would always stick around—often unnoticed. There were aspects of my personality that were keeping me in toxic friendships, prompting me to mold into the chameleon in the room to fit in, or sacrificing myself for "the greater good." I spiritually bypassed many moments in my life that were transformational opportunities because they scared the shit out of me. I saw periods of utter lack of self-worth, truly believing I was unlovable, and times when I put myself last so I wouldn't rock the boat for others around me.

Every single time I did this I felt my body respond with a tightness. I felt myself sink and slowly but surely disappeared into the background of my own life. Coming face-to-face with your own growth can feel confronting at times. Sometimes, it means confronting the shadows you've been carrying. They don't like being caught, and they'll make you work hard to let them go. Your spiritual journey might bring an awareness to the surface that feels like you're being called out by yourself. It can be confusing and bring about feelings of shame, leaving you asking: Is this really who I am? How long has this shadow been here? How long have I been this way? Why didn't I notice this sooner?

The aim is to discover these areas of yourself or life without it feeling so intense—as if life is forcing our hand to expose them. Your spiritual practice is your best friend during these times. You can always rely upon it to help keep you grounded. It will assist in helping these confronting moments not feel so charged up and will give you daily opportunities to regulate yourself, get still and settle, and discover what's hidden within.

Emotions are our greatest insight to our spiritual journey. They offer a brief window into the past, while guiding both you and the Seeker toward the next step in self-awareness and healing. In doing so, they cultivate a deeper inner wisdom to draw on in the future. If left unchecked or unregulated it can feel disorientating, like being tossed around in a storm. You might feel irritable, disconnected, restless, and insecure. Regulating your emotions is the piece that helps experiencing and feeling through them manageable, and a little easier to enjoy the spiritual ride. Your spiritual practice will be of great assistance in finding your anchor in otherwise rough seas.

I had the most momentum in my journey once I really understood what regulating your emotions meant. I was moving into my late twenties and thirties and really didn't know how to do this. I don't know when I missed that "emotional regulation" class throughout my life, no doubt I was caught in some daydream or looking out a window, or perhaps I wasn't taught how to do it at all.

I'd been working with children in my late twenties, and a very large portion of our days were talking about emotional regulation. The kids books were great, and I loved to see the children have access to them, but I needed something for adults. And because I was ready, my new teacher appeared.

Brené Brown became a superstar seemingly overnight with her TED Talk on vulnerability. If you've seen it you know why, and if you haven't please don't waste one more day without watching it. In her most recent book release, *Atlas of the Heart,* she provides descriptions of eighty-seven distinct emotions and experiences and how they shape our lives. She clarifies the differences between emotions that may feel similar to one another, removing the obstacle around struggling to identify emotions and increasing emotional vocabulary.

Emotional regulation is your ability to recognize, understand, and manage your emotions in a healthy and constructive way—especially in intense moments. It's a learned skill, and asks for consistent dedication to understanding emotions so that you can better connect with yourself and others. How can we regulate an emotion if we don't know what we are feeling? How do we sort through the mess of our feelings if some emotions feel similar to others yet have a different meaning? It's a complex series of trails that emotions can take you on. When emotions get activated they want to be identified, and in some cases are linked to experiences of our pasts, thus providing a link to further exploration on your spiritual journey. Emotions will say: Look at me. What am I? Where did I come from? Our emotions stay with us until we bring our awareness to them.

I was nearly thirty and re-entering the dating world for the first time after eight years of being in a relationship. It was 2018 and swipe culture was going strong. I hadn't been on a date in years. On one hand I found it exciting, and the other hand, it was terrifying to me. All it took was one date to fall apart for me to really feel the need for emotional regulation. It was time for me to take my new-found emotional intelligence out for a spin.

I'll set the scene. After a week of planning for a date, talking consistently and solidifying a plan, the day finally came. I was excited. Nervous. Filled with a little anticipation. Then nothing. I was left "on read" on the day of. I had been ghosted. Here we go... Emotions were activated and I was running high on adrenaline. Was it adrenaline, or was it something else? I felt like there was so much happening inside me. Thoughts and emotions were coming in fast and heavy. Activating all kinds of things within me.

Emotionally I was pissed, annoyed, disappointed. Physically I felt a wave of heat rolling over me, agitation seeping through my pores. There was so much happening emotionally and physically. At this point, I had been taking my spiritual practice pretty seriously and declared that I would not leave my meditation mat until I could untangle all those feelings.

This strong of a response from being ghosted didn't make sense. I barely knew this guy. I was more annoyed by my response than the actual ghosting. I sat down, buckled in for the ride, took a breath, and buckled down. An easy four count box breath. In for four, hold for four, out for four, and hold for four. What is this? What am I feeling? I would ask myself over and over. What's the root of this? Have I felt this before? The answer came to me clear as day. The emotion I was feeling was abandonment. Here I thought I was pissed that he just wasted my time. No, there was a whole lot more to it than that.

This ghosting experience activated abandonment within me. As soon as I identified the emotion I immediately felt calmer, and the heat in my body started to slowly subside. That calming and physical response confirmed for me that I was heading in the right direction with my reflection. My breathing became more at ease. I barely knew this guy, he didn't abandon me, but did I know abandonment? Absolutely.

At the beginning of this book I spoke about my childhood. I spoke about how I was pretty close with my dad until one day he moved, so we weren't any longer. That change in our relationship and dynamic had an effect on me. We had been close when I was younger. We planted those trees together. Went from chore to chore around our hobby farm together. We dreamed of the evolution of our family together. You can imagine then, that the change in living arrangements may have felt like abandonment to me. The root of this shadow was planted around that time. I imagine I felt forgotten, that I was suddenly not as important. But as a child, you don't have the words for it, so you bury it down until one day some random guy ghosts you and all of a sudden your inner child, teenager, or young adult version starts squirming because similar feelings have resurfaced. These periodic visitations from the past are keys to unveiling what the Seeker within is ready for you to move forward from. These triggered moments can be your greatest teachers if you seize the opportunity to work with it.

When I was on the mat, doing my box breathing and asking myself repeatedly what I was feeling and if I'd felt it before, it wasn't until I was able to identify the feeling that I was able to make sense of what I was experiencing. Once I did, I sat with it. I placed my hands on my heart and felt the emotion deeply, allowing it to move and surface. I acknowledged that it was there, and I knew exactly when I had felt it in the past. This ghosting made me feel like I wasn't important, and this resonated with similar feelings from my past.

When you're a kid you don't have names for all these emotions; you just feel them very deeply. Gabor Matè mentions in his work that trauma we carry isn't necessarily the event we went through, but how the event made us feel. Without regulating or working through the powerful emotions they can stay running through us until a similar experience comes along that reminds us of it. They are powerful and sometimes unforgettable. The feeling and the emotion are tied together. The initial emotional reaction will root itself in the mind, body and energy, and can become a root cause of later emotional and energetic dysregulation. When I asked, "Have I felt this before?" a light switched on. I didn't judge it or shame myself for feeling it. I simply acknowledged it.

In moments like this we can talk ourselves out of the healing work. Instead of buckling down, feeling, or working through it, we tell ourselves to get over it or that it wasn't that big of a deal. Rather than soothing ourselves by saying this—which is often why we do this, it can invalidate the part of ourselves asking for love. My [over]emotional response to being ghosted was my abandoned inner child coming forward and asking to be acknowledged and loved. When moments like this happen they are all glimpses into who we are. They are invitations to evolve spiritually—by embracing them, you unlock profound wisdom and joy. Ignoring them or labeling them as silly is turning away from the very growth your soul seeks and your Seeker is nudging you toward.

When you diminish your experience or the emotions rising to the surface, they don't go away. They go right back down inside, until one day it screams so loudly that you can no longer ignore it. I went on to journal immediately after this experience and my time on the mat, and still have the journal entry. It is so powerful to write when you are feeling waves of emotions or when feeling them intensely.

That day I journaled:

Did this person abandon you? *No, I don't even really know them.*

Have you felt abandoned in the past? *Yes, absolutely.*

Are you abandoned in this life? *No.*

Why? *Because I haven't abandoned myself, and if I haven't abandoned myself then I haven't abandoned God, and God hasn't abandoned me. That's all that matters.*

A moment of feeling abandoned—where in the past I'd have felt unwanted or unimportant, sneaking off to my bed to hide my tears and insecurities—transformed into a declaration of self-trust and the activation of a greater faith. Just like that, the roller coaster ride came to an end. I reminded myself that my relationship with my dad has taken years of work, and we are closer now than we've ever been. The jokes and laughter have returned tenfold. Although I never know if a text message is, in fact, a jump scare video, with him then receiving some choice words from me in return. Even though we've worked on our relationship and continue to grow together, echoes from the past can still rise to the surface. The work to be done often involves healing from past hurt, being present in the moment, and choosing differently for the future. I quickly collected myself and met my best friend at a new local restaurant, and as always, we had a blast together—laughing our way into the future and feeling a little lighter than before.

These are the kinds of revelations that can make their way out of your body and onto a page. It would not have happened if I acted in my original adrenaline-driven energy and produced an unhealthy action. I could have brought this emotionally-charged energy into the remaining part of my day and let it taint every new experience I got to have.

Emotional events like this have a possibility of flooding your body with so many chemicals that it alters your brain chemistry, dysregulates your nervous system, or even become a stage of your fears and insecurities to play out. Stepping in and regulating yourself is an act of self love as much as it is self advocacy for your right to live a meaningful life. The more you sit down and practice regulating your emotions, the quicker the process can happen.

What could have been an entire evening steeped in insecurities, up-set and frustration was transmuted into an opportunity for deeper heal-ing, a chance to build my confidence, and a reminder of my faith. The best part, I wasn't on my meditation mat for more than twenty minutes. It took just over ten minutes to buckle down, recognize and notice the emotion, then acknowledge it and regulate it. It doesn't have to take all day to heal aspects of your life, but it does need you to take notice and actively participate in your ability to regulate and heal from within.

I also could have just avoided the way I felt. I could have stuffed it down and pretended it didn't happen, I could have spiritually bypassed it away only for it to jump out and surprise me the next time something activated that response. Avoidance of what we are experiencing doesn't make it go away, it simply pauses the immediate response and then starts the cycle again, waiting for you to give it the attention it's so desperately wanting from you. The emotions and pains don't want to stay buried in-side. They want to come out, but can only do so with your attention and participation. Each time an event in the present triggers a deeper emo-tion from your past, you are given the opportunity to revisit the initial wounding—the root cause—and heal it. There is a strength in emotional regulation.

Each time you buckle in for the emotional ride, buckle down in your focused practice, and do the inner healing work, the shadow shrinks just a little bit more. Until one day, it's gone for good. That makes all the work you've done, the focused efforts you've put in, and dips and dives you've felt your way through worth every single second it took to get there.

As you move along on this journey you'll see unhealed emotional wounds more clearly every day—in yourself and in others. You'll begin to notice people tossing unrealistic expectations on to the next person without even knowing they are doing it. People all around you are at completely different levels of self awareness, and we do ourselves a disser-vice by comparing ourselves to another, or wishing they were somewhere along the journey that they are not. We are all at different progressions in our own journeys, and comparison acts as quicksand on this grand adventure of yours. We also do a disservice to ourselves when we succumb to their state of being and fall into it with them. Before we know it we've matched their energy, mimicking their drama back to them, our bodies becoming entangled in the mess. Notice where they are at and empathize, but still hold your own space and discipline on your state of being.

Just as you're becoming more aware of yourself and those around you, there are some people in this world that have developed their level of self awareness so well that they can notice your state of being before you can. There are blindspots that exist within us all. As your circles grow and you meet others who you trust and build a genuine connection with, grant them the space to share what they see. Be open to feedback from them about things you may not have noticed within yourself yet. These are your teachers. Hold these people close because they will assist in you creating a more present and meaningful life where the best version of yourself is available.

Please remember that while you've decided to take the spiritual path not everyone wants to go with you or match the speed that you're setting. Let someone's North be your South, and let each take the paths that feel right to them. This is your own ride, and it's one you can enjoy along the way, laugh at all the dips and turns, and know that you've got your own back and are buckled in tight for the ride.

Chapter Eight

PEACEFUL TRANSITIONS

The decision to embark on a spiritual path seems to happen over-night. It's like you went to bed one night as one person and then woke up the next morning feeling like a different person. Some even call it an awakening. So what do we do when we wake up different but the world around us stays the same? Do we demand everyone else has a corresponding awakening? Do we abruptly shut others out before even finishing breakfast? What do we do if we want to salvage or heal the relationships in our lives, and is it even possible to do that when you awaken feeling like a totally different person? The answer to all those questions will be determined by how you choose to move forward.

The habit of walking on eggshells is something that I have done consistently over my life. I would temper my words to keep the peace or manage other people's emotions. I would prioritize the happiness and desires of others over my own. You will find, as my Seeker has shown me, that the habit of walking on eggshells doesn't really benefit anyone. I want to encourage you to put the eggshells in the garbage, or compost, depending on your preference. The most underutilized and forgotten tool people have available to use on their spiritual journey is communication. I have seen people so paralyzed by fear of using their voice because they were scared of what they would receive in return, essentially walking on egg-shells to avoid any unpleasantness, judgment, or even violence. This was me. I had been on the receiving end of powerful words and forces in my life, and it created this deep fear that if I spoke up, or spoke the truth, I could be hurt or that I would upset someone.

To be able to articulate yourself and speak from a place with open dialogue and respect is a skillset that isn't spoken about enough. The ability to communicate with another seems to be placed so far down on the priority list that we've grown accustomed to not knowing how to talk to one another—or ourselves, for that matter. Sharpening your communication skills can help you transition more easefully into your spiritual journey.

If we neglect to work on our communication skills, we can take things too personally, speak rashly or disrespectfully, or miss out on being able to speak or listen deeply and authentically. Instead of communicating a fear or vulnerability we may avoid people or disappear from someone's life completely. Once you've assessed your circles and the people you have in your life and decided who is aligned, you'll be able to speak with them openly and clearly about what you're experiencing and choosing to do. Doing so will help everyone involved feel more comfortable with the changes that will be coming in your life.

The way we communicate with one another starts with one thing: emotions. The need to regulate your emotions will come up again and again. Your emotions will determine the way you enter a conversation, either combatively or compassionately, both are entirely your choice. Relationships and friendships have ended prematurely, in my opinion, because neither party knew how to speak or listen to the other. So to maintain your relationships, focus on regulating your emotions and being intentional with your communication.

As you begin to discover who you are and who you want to be, you'll notice the areas in your life where you feel some resistance or hesitation. You may start feeling resistance towards a friend or family member or even your job. What used to be covered by smog is now clearly visible and you may find that you're resisting spending time with them or hesitating making a change because you know it will be disruptive. This clarity can bring with it heightened and potentially, confronting emotions. The Seeker within you will be guiding you through this. Pay attention to the resistance and hesitation, and the resulting emotions that surface, as this clarity comes in for you.

Seeing aspects of our lives that were created in the masquerade and have grown into dysfunction can be a lot to process all at one time, so patience with yourself and others will be your ally on your spiritual journey. You don't need to overhaul everything overnight. You can gently notice the resistance and hesitation, notice where you're feeling like a change may be needed, and ease your way into it. And remember, just because you've chosen to begin prioritizing and valuing spirituality doesn't mean the people around you have, as well.

It can feel exhilarating learning so much about yourself and the world around you that you are filled with the desire to share your new-found knowledge with others. You'll want to run to your friends and family and share this thing that absolutely blew your mind or that you discovered about your shared relationship. But caution is needed here. What may be clear to you may not be clear to others. It is not your responsibility to dictate to others their blind spots or dysfunction unless they are intentionally asking you for it. If you've ever been on the receiving end of unsolicited advice then you know how it feels. I have found that it is best that when sharing your new discoveries, to share them from your perspective and experience only. What you learned and how it relates to your life and evolution. If they are interested in learning more from you, they will ask and the space for your feedback will be created.

The spiritual journey and the Seeker within has one agenda: connect you more deeply to yourself, others, and the world around you. This will inevitably lead to hard conversations at times. This is where intentional, clear communication and emotional regulation is absolutely golden on your journey. It can give a conversation a better chance to be filled with compassion and mutual respect rather than one that ends in a literal or metaphorical door being slammed shut. With the former, you can be constructive and work towards a more meaningful connection, and with the latter, you can leave behind you a trail of unnecessary vindictiveness and pain.

At the beginning of your spiritual journey you may notice that you begin to subconsciously unload years of frustration onto others—forgetting the one thing spirituality always asks of us: take ownership. We must take ownership of our own behaviour, our own actions, and the way we've lived. We have to own how we've helped create the world around us. Everyone else is not the problem. "You create your own reality" is a phrase you'll hear often on your spiritual journey. For example: If you allow someone to speak to you a certain way, or take advantage of you without speaking up for yourself or confronting the behaviour, don't be surprised if it keeps on happening. It's now an expected way of interacting with you, you are the one who gives them permission by allowing it to continue. Own it, then change it #sorrynotsorry.

When we own our behaviour we own our present circumstances. Through ownership we bring light to decisions that we made in fear or lack, and we bring to present the reality of our choices. When we take accountability for what's not working for *us* rather than tossing blame onto *others*, it can mitigate any defensiveness that the other person may feel if you went into the conversation from a space of attack or confrontation. If it's initiated in aggressive energy—regardless of its intention—it will be responded to in defense. Make sure you're approaching conversations with communication and actions that match your intentions. Get clear on your intentions first, and then approach the other person with compassion and kindness.

You may also find yourself ready to have a conversation with someone who seems to have a firm grasp of the spiritual journey. You can tell they've done the work. They feel like a walking example of someone committed to their journey and they practice what they preach. Someone who can show you the patience and ease that you'd find in a constructive open conversation. *This,* is holding space. Sitting down with someone to share what you're battling can reap profound benefits if both parties are willing to speak with honesty and actively listen to the other. If you're looking for emotional support from someone who's not in touch with their emotions, or empathy from unempathetic people, don't be surprised if the outcome isn't as you desire.

As you grow spiritually you will notice changes in the dynamics of the relationships around you, but you can navigate them with grace if you choose. Look at who and what you are surrounded by. With your spiritual practice to ground you, be honest with yourself with which connections are the most meaningful and which ones no longer serve your higher potential. The dynamic is what is important, not necessarily the interests. It's common for people to have different interests, yet still be a meaningful person in someone's life. If the differences outweigh what you're willing to accept, then a conversation needs to be had or a boundary needs to be set.

It's important to acknowledge that those you previously shared a similar interest with may not follow you on your new journey, and sometimes connections will dissolve. You must trust that you can handle the stresses or uncertainties of the inevitability of what changing your life may result in. You may find yourself with fewer friends, different interests, and spending more time on new priorities and your growth. You may begin to be up earlier and out late less. You may trade reality shows for the gym and find happiness in solitude rather than among groups of people.

You also get to find compromise if you're willing to transform your connections. It doesn't always have to be a binary decision, as-is or not at all. Should you find yourself looking at a connection that you hold with respect, yet notice you're feeling called towards different activities, then you can find new ways to spend time together. Maybe a couple times a month you stay out late with a friend versus stopping those late-nights completely. Work together and find some common ground, and be honest with the people who mean a lot to you. Should they not respect how you're feeling and where you're at, then use it as an opportunity to appreciate the clarity they've shown in your connection and, with acceptance and conviction, move on.

Be honest with yourself and be very intentional with the connections that you choose to invest in. Learn how to advocate for yourself and how to communicate with others effectively. If your connections are meaningful yet challenging, practice patience and compassion for yourself and the other person. If they are willing to honour your spiritual journey and what you are needing at this time, take a moment of gratitude.

A spiritual life can feel like a lonely life at times, but the connections that we nurture and nurture us in return, are some of the greatest gifts you'll get to experience. I once heard this quote and to me it spoke of the possibility of longevity in relationships: "This person has seen and loved all versions of me, and they will be with me in the end." There is trust and faith in each other in that statement.

You can walk this journey with others, or you can walk alone for a while—both are valid. But either way, you always have the power to build bridges with intention, grace, and love. You can ease into your spiritual journey and transition your relationships peacefully. And that, too, is a spiritual practice worth committing to.

Chapter Nine

THE UNOFFICIAL BODYGUARD

The ego. Some say it's not worth defending. That it makes everything more difficult, but I believe it deserves its due. It works tirelessly, rarely going down without a fight. *You have to respect the work ethic.* Though, it does require you to help keep it in check because if you don't, likely someone else will. Left unchecked it will run wild, picking up momentum like a boulder speeding downhill heading towards destruction. I'm talking about the ego—the powerful part of our psyche that's evolved from a lifetime of experiences both good and bad. It picks and chooses what it likes, and it will embellish or belittle those things depending on how it feels that day and what outcomes it truly wants. It can be sneaky and sly, always wanting the upper hand.

From my experience there are two main motivations of the ego. One is to keep you safe and the other to make you feel right, about everything, all the time. The spiritual journey naturally sparks a growth in self-awareness. Except the ego doesn't want you to be self aware. It wants to control your actions and reactions and ultimately be the one calling the shots. "Trust me," it says, "I'll take care of this," it assures you. We talked about discernment earlier, and if there is one place that discernment is required, it's in working with the ego.

Giving our decision making over to the ego can happen within seconds. It's a knee-jerk-reaction and the ego will never stop you from handing over to it your better judgement. It's our self-awareness that turns on the slow motion responses and makes room for reasonable and reflective thinking rather than impulsive, habitual thinking. Becoming observant when your ego turns on, and consistently practicing and being curious about its behaviour, will undoubtedly accelerate your journey and create more room for fulfillment and spiritual growth.

The book *The Untethered Soul* by Michael A. Singer was, and has continued to be, a staple in my book collection for spirituality. He speaks to the "observer"—a similar inner wisdom to what I call the Seeker. The observer, according to Singer, encourages us to take time each day to get into observer-mode as if you are looking at yourself from a few feet away. It's the part of us that watches, not reacts. The Seeker within wants you to be curious about your behaviours, discover where patterns are rooted, and celebrate with you as you detach from old ways of being. With ego out of the way, our higher awareness can identify the emotions, fears, shadows, inspirations, insecurities, and vulnerabilities you are currently holding. If you allowed your awareness to shine upon yourself, what would you see?

The ego hates to be found out. It believes that its vulnerabilities are a weakness, and guards them fiercely, refusing to be preyed upon. It will always choose to be the predator and the top of the chain is where it wants to stay. The more you give over to it the harder it may become to break free from the grasp it has on you. The ego, in other words, is absolutely scared shitless hanging on for dear life in an effort to keep itself, and therefore you, safe from any possible harm. The more self-aware you become the less the ego gets to call the shots, and it doesn't like that at all. It won't go down without a fight. The Seeker within sees through fear and the blind efforts of the ego to the possibility of something more

Rather than fight your ego, I propose having a conversation with it—forming a partnership. This conversation with your ego is an ongoing one. It gets to be infused with compassion and patience along the way. Up until the moment you decided to begin your spiritual journey your ego has acted separately from your awareness. It's been stealth in its actions, but now gets to be brought in to work with you collaboratively. As you continue to practice working alongside your ego it will test you, and just like you are creating a new habit of awareness, the ego is developing new habits of its own.

We've all met that one person whose ego is inflated. You know, the ones who can't wait to tell everyone how well they are doing, and how successful they are even when nobody asked. Everything is always, or needs to be, about them. The ego loves external validation and their ego has taken over. But notice as this is happening, our own ego arrogantly wants to judge or dismiss them and what they're saying. Two egos have now entered the conversation and it's going nowhere. It is devoid of any connection. If we slow it down, we can see that their ego was running the show for them, and our ego didn't like it one bit.

In your excitement to begin your spiritual journey, you might have become flooded with a newfound lightness and sense of upliftment in your life. In the process, you may have told friends or family you were making a change—an announcement that may have been met with hurtful judgement, making for a not-so-peaceful transition. In turn, the ego, feeling threatened, responded to that judgement with defensiveness. It was ego versus ego on the path to spirituality. Never a great beginning.

This is why I encourage you to check in with your ego on a regular basis. If we stand confidently in our authenticity without expectation or need of validation from others, then our spiritual life can thrive. Cultivating acceptance of scenarios and ourselves naturally quiets the ego resulting in more peace and joy in life. The ego becomes less of a dictator and more of a companion on your spiritual journey.

Before I knew the role the ego was playing in my life, it was working hard to protect me and make me, it, right. This is never a good situation to be in, but perhaps even more tumultuous when in a relationship with someone. Successful relationships don't keep a tally on who is right and who is wrong. But when the ego is involved, there is always someone who is right and the other person is most definitely wrong. It makes the relationship feel transactional, not equal or mutually respectful.

I had been in a relationship for about eight years and I found myself looking in the mirror and not recognizing myself. As I looked at the person in the mirror my ego started to stir. It was ready for the blame and rage game, bringing me down with it. Resentment coursed through my veins and seeped into every aspect of my life. My ego was blaming my emotional state, my utter lack of recognition, on everything and everyone else. It would consistently tell me that I was doing my best for everyone and, in return, everyone was doing the bare minimum for me. It was saying that I wasted the best childbearing years of my life for someone who had no intentions of being with me long-term. This wasn't entirely a false statement, but I had some responsibility to own as well.

I hadn't learned how to set boundaries with others yet and the lack of boundaries created a clear path for the ego to commandeer my thinking. I was deeply unhappy so the ego made it everyone else's fault. My ego fought hard for me. As a response, my demeanor became mean, critical, and despondent towards others, especially my partner. I meditated to find peace, I journaled to find clarity, and tried repeatedly to communicate to my partner. In the end I always felt unheard, misdirected, dismissed, and the worst of all, unlovable.

The tide turned when I found mentors. I knew I couldn't keep going on my own. I had allowed my ego to run the show for so long. My spiritual practice wasn't helping me enough on its own. I had come to rely upon my spiritual practice, but things felt so uncertain and deeply emotional that I knew I needed more help. I didn't know where to turn. I didn't want to be passive or fall further into despair. Instead, I took a chance on myself.

I knew that it was now or never and got myself the support I needed. Ego said, "That money could be spent elsewhere," and my Seeker within said, "We need some help here." Sometimes, when you live in a darker place for a long time, you may need the help of an extended hand—with no other intention than to lift you up or help find the threads of joy or hope to carry you through. That helping hand provided mentorship in my thought process and helped me re-discover the version of myself that I looked up to and reminded me who I wanted to be.

It took some time to cross paths with the right coaches, but I knew I needed it so I kept going. Things began to come into focus once I found them. I started seeing past the anger-filled illusion that my ego said was my life, and slowly brought my focus back to myself. I knew I desperately needed help so I relied upon my discernment and perseverance to help me override every time my ego wanted to jump in and tell me to stop. When life gets intense, and your spiritual practice isn't supportive enough, your ego will quickly step in and try to protect you. But the kind of guarding that the ego is equipped for isn't what you want. It's focused externally whereas you want internal healing. So, keep looking for the support you need. You deserve great care.

I was living in my inflated ego, within a blind spot of my own making. Even after all of the spiritual work I had done I couldn't see that I had been forcing a life into being that wasn't meant to be. I was letting my ego run wild. My inner Seeker wanted me to discover love for myself again, stop pretending, drop the masks and tell the truth. Meanwhile my ego was fighting for me to be seen, cherished, and prioritized by my partner. You can't fault the ego for fighting for you—it is your companion after all—but you can ask yourself: Who's speaking right now? If it's the ego instead of your Higher Self, then you get to come to the front of the line and be the one speaking for yourself first.

My ego didn't want to give up and it was highly competitive. It was trying to keep me in a cycle or find someone to blame for what it felt was a failure. It kept bringing questions forward: Why does everyone assume I'm always okay? Why would they think that behaviour towards me was acceptable? Why does my partner not step up and stand up for me?

The ego always wants answers and the Seeker within accepts that you may not always get them. The ego clings to keep things together where it feels it has put in all its efforts and will not easily let go. Higher awareness and the Seeker know that trusting yourself, believing in your resiliency and ability to adapt will far outweigh any need to be validated by another. Challenges that arise in your life may feel like a threat to the ego while at the same time, the Seeker understands that those same challenges are tied to growth and change.

The Seeker within was encouraging me to take a chance on addressing deeper subconscious behaviours that were continuing to hold me back. I had been staying in a relationship where I felt last on a priority list, which left me feeling unimportant and forgotten. My goals for being a wife and mother kept getting put to the side, yet I continued to stay for years. Through mentorship, I began to understand the power of self love, believing in your worth and value in relationships, and invoking the power from within to walk away from what's not right for you. It took me surpassing the will of my ego to get to this point though. The ego doesn't play the game of reflection, and it's very good at distracting you from doing all that work. It may even try to distract you for multiple years of our life, or even a lifetime.

The scariest word of all that you could say to the ego is the word change. It's uncharted territory and it will immediately come up with any excuse or reason to not jump into the unknown. The ego gets scared and wants to keep you exactly where you are, and the Seeker encourages you to live, experience, and expand—change. The pull between the two can feel as if you're in the middle of a tug of war between two strong forces, and feeling caught in the middle can feel uncomfortable and exhausting. The duality of these two forces will always exist, and it's your free will and courage that dictates the choices you make. Your ego will give over to your Higher Self when you tell it to trust you. This is the importance of learning to work alongside your ego rather than fight against it.

If you are on the edge of taking a chance at something new, but have been too scared to take action, it's likely your ego is calling the shots. Remember, change, no matter how big or small, is not something the ego ever wants to do. Believing that you can handle whatever comes your way when taking a leap of faith will help quiet the ego and will benefit your growth.

If you've recently grown leaps and bounds from where you've started, and are feeling fatigue from the growth you've made, be mindful to rest but don't give up. When we expand or feel as if we are stretching beyond our limitations you may want to stop, but these are the moments when you stand on the edge of your greatest growth. We are here to learn, and to live our lives fully. The coexistence of your ego and your Seeker will inevitably breed fatigue on occasion, and it's important to remember this and persevere. Ask yourself this question when you feel you're on the brink: Am I fearing and stalling my growth or surrendering to it?

The ego in its weird and wacky way just wants to keep you safe. It's doing its job if it's protecting you from all angles, but it wasn't given the job to stop you from living your life to the fullest. It's no villain. It's more like a bodyguard, albeit a misguided one.

Sometimes it needs attention and a little reassurance. Work with it, not against it and you may find your confidence soar. Nobody knows you like your ego, it's been with you all your life. So bring it along for the rest of the ride and show it a good time. It may be the partner you need to help you keep going when you feel tired and contemplate giving up. It may also be there to remind you one day that you've done more than you give yourself credit for. Let your ego be the unofficial bodyguard—not the boss. Let it walk alongside you, not in front of you. A day will come when you see it cheering you on instead of holding you back, it's then that you'll know you're walking your path in your spiritual journey with both courage and grace.

Chapter Ten

THE HUMP

I had been putting my feet to the pavement for well over an hour now. The mist in the air had subsided the further I got away from Niagara Falls, and I was coming up on kilometer marker fourteen. It was my third half marathon within a year, and the one I trained the hardest for. My dog Mercedes was my running partner during training, and would keep me going when I felt like giving up. She couldn't be with me in this race, and depending on her to pull me when I lagged behind my time, wasn't something I could fall back on. Within a few more kilometers I knew I would likely hit my runner's wall, but assumed I'd be close enough to the finish line that I could push right through. A runner's wall is a moment during a run when you regret every decision you've ever made about running, question why you decided to sign up for this torture race to begin with, and wonder if anyone will notice if you just bow out of the damn thing now. It was my fifth half marathon within a couple of years and every time I ran one, I hit a wall—every single time. Knowing it could happen and that I had experienced it in other races helped me mentally prepare for what I knew was coming soon.

With each mile marker the end was coming closer to view, and I knew that we would round the bend to the final stretch within the next forty minutes. I was pumped. I had a new personal best time goal, and I was on track to hit it. It would be close but I could do it. The one thing I forgot about the wall though is that it comes completely out of nowhere. Once I noted my time and noted my goal progression I was promptly humbled by the wall. I still had about six or seven kilometers to go at this point, and everything started to ache. Cramps came darting into my sides like razor blades trying to escape from within me, and I could barely catch my breath let alone keep it rhythmic and strong. My knees felt like they were constantly wanting to hyper extend and I could barely keep a single stride in order. I wasn't expecting to hit a wall yet, and the humidity of Niagara Falls in the summer started to affect my mindset.

I made the decision to walk for a little bit, take some time and catch my breath. I fought so hard against this because sometimes when you start walking it's hard to get moving again. The muscles start to seize up, and it feels like it takes even more effort to get momentum back. I knew I was close to the end of the race, and quitting wasn't an option for me. I gave myself the reprieve and started to run again, and within about ten minutes I was walking again. My muscles seized up like the last time, and my knees felt like they were on fire. "Why did I willingly sign up for this torture? This wasn't supposed to happen yet." These thoughts came rushing into my mind. I caught a glimpse of another runner who quit the race walking along the pedestrian path that's set just off the parkway that we were running. I wondered if anyone would care if I bailed out of this thing because it was feeling worse and worse with each time the soles of my shoes hit the road. Self-doubt and the self-imposed pressure of perfection were firing on all cylinders and battling one another.

As I came over the final hill signalling the last stretch, the outpour of support from the crowd was invigorating. There was a small Tim Hortons on the corner, and some people were even offering out little Timbits, bite-sized dough rounds, for the runners. A little sugar boost courtesy of your local donut shop. I had a good laugh, used the decline of the hill for some momentum, and enriched my soul with the cheers from the folks calling my name and offering their encouragement. And yes, I took a Timbit—a nice fresh chocolate glazed. Mmmm...

Complete strangers took the time to read my name tag on my race bib, cheered me on, and reminded me that the race was coming to end. It was just what I needed. The wall disappeared and as I came into the last two kilometers I saw my younger cousin Colin on the side of the road ready to run along with me closer to the finish line. We shared the experience of the race with the beautiful scene of the power and majestic roar from Niagara Falls as the backdrop. He left me at the final stretch and I raced myself in towards the finish line. There were so many people there cheering me on, and I tried to catch their eyes as I crossed the final mat, and heard the beep that signals the completion of my race and dictates my final time. I ended up being three minutes over my goal time, but it was still a personal best. It was still an accomplishment because I never gave up, and did the absolute best I could. I persevered and crossed the finish line. I overcame the wall, and I was elated.

In reflection, the race was metaphorical to my spiritual journey. There have been moments along the way where I felt as if I hit a growth wall. After grieving old friends, old relationships, and processing the emotional weight of countless patterns driven by my ego, I felt exhausted. My spiritual journey has sometimes invoked the similar questions I asked myself on that race day: Why did I do this?, How much more could there be? This was my ego still clinging to security, hating the unknowing of what was to come, and begging for a sense of normalcy wanting me to stop.

This is what I call "The Hump." It's a moment in our journey where we feel the exhaustion of climbing some invisible hill. We begin to feel more fatigue than joy and wonder if we should keep going or just stop. It's also the place where the largest and most life altering transformation occurs. The hump does come to an end and like Napoleon Hill says, "You're only three feet from gold." To give up now has you stopping mere moments from your greatest growth. The fatigue felt within the hump is the brain's expansion into new territory, building new connections, and waiting for your final declaration to keep going so that it can continue to grow.

I have experienced many humps. Each time I came upon one I would almost forget the one that happened before. Like signing up for another half-marathon completely forgetting how much struggle the previous one brought. This is why I believe your spiritual practice is critical. It allows you to look back on how far you've come and not forget the work you've put in. Everything you've experienced before, and the bravery you've shown in your decision making is your training for whatever comes next. It strengthens the muscles of your intuition, courage, and trust within yourself. Your spiritual growth and practice are your Seeker's training tools for life. The spiritual journey is an endurance race, a marathon—not a sprint.

There may come a time when you hit a wall. You may even be in one now. It feels like spiritual fatigue. The best way forward is to give yourself permission to take baby steps—to essentially walk during your marathon. You may feel you need to take a step back, recoup some energy, and then carry on. That is perfectly okay.

And while you're taking a step back, make time for some play. Your spiritual journey doesn't have to feel like, or actually be, work all the time. You get to have fun too. A marathon isn't lacking in its entertainment. Bands, solo singers, DJs, and noisemakers pave the way to the finish line. Playfulness can help keep your cup half full if you feel you're heading towards empty, so infuse some joy and fun along the way. In some cases, it can be the greatest catalyst for some momentum.

It is so easy to become discouraged on our spiritual journey. Constantly uncovering, reflecting, and evolving can take a toll on us. It can become all work, exhausting work at that. Playfulness isn't a detour from spiritual growth—it's a fuel source. A trip to the beach, snapping shots of beautiful scenery, catching a live band, sharing a laugh at a local comedy show, or a night at the movies can sometimes bring us farther along on our spiritual journey than a thousand journal entries.

Playing and taking a step back can remind you that your journey will unfold and everything that needs to be revealed to you will be in divine time. There is no need to become an archeologist of your soul frantically excavating the next buried belief. Beware of any control constructs that the ego is subtly throwing in there. Don't try to "be the best" at healing. Don't compare yourself to others. The Seeker within knows that when you are ready the teacher will show up. When you are ready the next phase of your healing or journey will come into focus. There is no need to force or push on your journey. And when you hit a spiritual wall, pull back from the heaviness you may be experiencing and find something joyful and relaxing to do. It will feel like a balm to your heart and soul.

Trust that your spiritual practice and blossoming connection to your Seeker within will provide the signs and signals necessary for your next phase of growth, without you having to try to control the process. Trust yourself that you will become aware of it, thrive through it, or overcome any obstacle that may come next. There is no need to dig, scrape, or claw your way to enlightenment. What you are meant to learn next will naturally arise, so trust that what's meant to happen will happen—in divine timing.

Each hump will come with a different timeline of completion. You may overcome some humps quicker than others, and some may ask you for more patience than the last hump you persevered through. You may find you need more solitary time to reflect and be in your practice, and other times you may need community and support. The way through won't always be the same, but you can rely on your fundamental spiritual tools to help you. If you rush your way out of healing you may miss the key points requiring your attention, and if you don't see them now, they will reappear for you in the future. So slow down, pull back when you need to, and pay attention to where you're being guided.

In the hump, when you're struggling to keep going is exactly when you get to lock in and forge something sacred within yourself. That endurance doesn't just help you endure the hump, it helps you evolve along your spiritual journey. If you're in a hump, you're evolving.

In many spiritual and personal development workshops I've attended, I've shared this frustration of feeling like I'm learning the same lesson over and over and I don't understand why. I wasn't alone in that feeling. A lesson will remain in a cyclical pattern until we complete it fully. It's often compared to the layers of an onion, and while the lesson may feel similar, the depth of it is not. As you strengthen your confidence and trust within yourself, your awareness will pick up a deeper level of the same lesson. When you're in the middle of processing emotions and regulating yourself, it can feel like a similar pattern, but I can bet there is a depth and wisdom that wasn't there before. Sometimes you need to reflect back to see how far you've come and how, in hindsight, the earlier lessons may seem a lot easier now.

That marathon at Niagara Falls was my last one. While I hit a personal best for the race, I was also at a personal low. I had been in a relationship for a long time, and had spent most of my training hours visualizing a different outcome. I saw people get engaged after a race, and romanticized it a lot during the training phase for this particular race in Niagara. I had built a life there with him and his family, so I believed it certainly should be coming soon right? I was using the tools from the book *The Secret* trying to manifest my destiny. The book is focused on The Law of Attraction, teaching you to think about what you want to manifest into your life, and then feel how you want to feel when you get this outcome. Each training run would end with this "moment" of becoming engaged at the finish line being replayed in my mind and body. I kept the visual clear in my mind, and would finish my race trying to embody what it would feel like to get engaged. The end of the race came, and no engagement. I was gutted.

What *The Secret* didn't teach me—or maybe I selectively ignored it—was that you can't manifest your way to alignment if you're busy putting effort into misalignment. You have to feel it. Heal it. And sometimes, release it completely. Maybe I was trying to manifest something that wasn't meant to show up on my spiritual path.

The years between 2012 when I first moved to Niagara through to the summer of 2015, went by in a flash. I had officially given up on the idea that I may ever get married. Maybe marriage just wasn't in the cards for me, and in that divine moment of acceptance during a hump, something new came into my life.

I had recently been laid off from a job during a restructuring and found something to do at home online. While I was working I was listening to audios on YouTube about energy, which then led to another playing in the background as I worked away. It mentioned that Polarity Therapy could help people ground their energy. I'll never forget how quickly that caught my attention. I had heard of other alternative energy therapies before, but I had never heard of Polarity Therapy. That reflex, that immediate pull of my attention, was similar to the night at the bookshelf when I was drawn to *Soul's Perfection.*

I spent my time researching Polarity and its Eastern and Western in-fluence. It looked like a blend of the two worlds and provided a deeper understanding of energy systems. Terms like chakras came up, connecting the dots of information I read through the years. Polarity also introduced me to Ayurveda and Ayurvedic medicine. I was fascinated. My curiosity piqued with excitement and Polarity Therapy would now become my place of focus. While in the hump of wondering what was next for me and releasing my attachments to old dreams left unfulfilled, I kept moving. I didn't force anything. I allowed myself to be curious about new interests, and when something came into my energy field that felt good, I followed it. I was ready for something new, and the teacher arrived.

I had no idea at the time how important following this curiosity would become for me. This new discovery would completely change the way that I look at my life and the people around me. It would expand my understanding of the human body and its energy systems. It would allow me to deepen my spiritual practice even further, and help me experience life in a holistic way. It felt as if all of the work I'd put into my personal growth, a lifetime of listening to the Seeker within me, all of the failures I endured, and pivots I made in my life, had led me here. It led me to letting go of control, not forcing results into being that weren't meant to be, and opened my curiosity up to something new in my life. Dr. Wayne Dyer calls these moments "The Shift". If you're hearing a new inspiration now, or a call towards a new direction in life, there's probably a shift heading your way. So if you're feeling stuck, tired, or unsure—stay close to your Seeker. The shift might already be on its way, and is waiting on the other side of the hump, like Polarity was waiting for me.

Chapter Eleven

DISCOVERING THE HOLISTIC HUMAN

Ifinished my final race, excited and emotionally drained, and tragedy struck hard a few years after. Someone very close to me ended his life. It left this huge hole in my heart and while my faith in the afterlife helped me feel secure that he was okay now, it also forced me into support-mode for those around me who were also very close to him. The words of author Stephen Covey would often ring through my head: *Focus on what you can control.* This period was a time when I felt in control of very little.

I had big questions about his passing that couldn't be answered. I'd often reflect on our connection to each other and replay past conversations over and over again. I hadn't yet learnt how to hold space for people who were struggling with mental illness and addiction. Not only did this life altering experience inspire me to learn how to hold space for someone, it was an opportunity for my own healing around guilt, personal responsibility for someone else's actions, and self-forgiveness.

We aren't born knowing how to hold space for people who are dealing with something heavy in their life or suffering, but I knew that I wanted to learn. Not to hold myself responsible for someone's actions, but to perhaps be a safe space for them to express what they're feeling and have someone hold them through their experience and potential healing. Learning how to hold space for ourselves and others is such an important part of being a compassionate and empathetic person so I'll advocate until my final days that we can always become someone who can. We can always build more skills within ourselves to hold space for people who are struggling—your efforts to learn may save a life or inspire one to continue.

Still, intrusive thoughts were overloading my brain—and subsequently my body—so I focused on what I could do, what I could control. *Focus on what you can control.* I knew I could make a pot of coffee, plate some cheese and crackers, do the dishes, pick up groceries, and help host for a grieving mom and her visitors. Rinse and repeat. While pouring coffee or driving to the store, I'd tell myself to: "Breathe. Ride the emotional wave. Just keep moving." This was the beginning of me learning how to hold space for myself as well as the people around me—not just to focus on them, but to give myself what I needed, too.

I had been let go from my job, was physically feeling the wear and tear from the marathon training and runs I had completed over the years, and I was living hours away from my own family, only having my boyfriend and his family nearby. The way I grieved felt different from others. My spiritual beliefs kept me strong and moving forward, while others withdrew from the world, lost in mourning. The grief was heavy. All around me were people in deep sorrow. I did what I could to support them, taking care not to be insensitive to their personal grieving process while honouring my own. Life had just shattered for people I loved, but I held my own faith close and tried to keep moving forward. August 19th, my birthday, and his day of passing, will always be one of the most meaningful and sorrowful days of my life.

There's a card in the traditional tarot deck called The Tower. The visual is of a building on fire, and two people falling from the wreckage. I used to believe that this was a card to fear, but I've learned to understand that life, sometimes unexpectedly, requires a rebuild. I felt that everything in my life was falling apart regardless of how hard I tried to hold on to it.

I went to a local intuitive and medium named Jennifer Miller-McKenzie in Welland, ON. Someone who I trusted deeply, and was hoping could connect me to my late soul brother who had taken his life. In an emotional, tear-filled exchange of love and forgiveness, I healed a little bit, cried a lot, and felt a little bit of closure. We moved on to discussing my future, and she shared her intuitive insights. I told her of my sense that everything felt like it was falling apart and was wondering what was next. She began her reading and we spoke a bit about the energy work I was already doing, but elevating it to a different level. There was mention of working with anatomy and physiology, but not in the traditional sense of kinesiology. This was something that blended energy and physiology, but we couldn't find the word for it. Something in the back of my mind reminded me of the energy practice I had been researching months prior. The Seeker within took notice, and I knew what I would do immediately when I got home. I recognized this feeling... a sudden, excited urge. Momentum had returned to my life.

I went to my home office and found the Polarity Therapy research I'd done. I had almost forgotten about it because it was just something that caught my interest at the time but nothing came of it. And there it was, a tug in my mind that this was what we had been talking about—the blending of energy and physiology. Polarity Therapy is a fusion of East meets West energy medicine with a large emphasis on anatomy and physiology. It asserts that a human's overall wellness comes from a combination of forces. The idea that your thoughts, movement, energy balancing, nutrition, and working with the muscular tissues and fascia combined influenced your overall health.

The more I read on Polarity the more intrigued I became. This was where my Seeker was guiding me next. It felt monumental. This holistic approach to wellness was exactly what I was searching for in my life. I had grown up with the Canadian Food Guide, BMI scores, diet culture and exercise metrics, but the thought process and the subtlety of the tissues of our body was new and exciting for me. It taught me that I could eat nourishing foods, train and run half-marathons, and do my meditations and journaling, but my fears were still present within my subconscious and they activated stress hormones and tension within me.

Polarity Therapy states that each person has a unique energy system—the Wireless Anatomy of Man—that is affected by their life experiences, current daily choices, and thoughts which produce a result in the mind and body. I continued to learn that wellness isn't only about the food we eat and the exercises we do, but how various areas of our life contribute to our overall health. I was learning that the building of health and wellness can be achieved through a series of gentle yet powerful bodywork sequences, polarizing energy currents within the body, a change in thought process, emphasis on nutrition, and specific movements.

As I read more about Polarity Therapy I no longer felt like everything was falling apart. I didn't notice any of the grief or the emotional roller coaster I had been on, and was solely focusing on my new interest and how I could find a practitioner in the area. It was as if I had blinders on, keeping me focused on one direction—forward. I found David Pinto in Toronto, ON, not too far from where I was living in Niagara but far enough that I could have made an excuse not to go. Three years had passed from my marathon, but I was still feeling the tension in my muscles that hadn't gone away, so I wanted to give this Polarity thing a try. My aching body was enough to inspire me to book an appointment regardless of the distance.

Turns out, nothing could stop me from going. Knowing I'd be driving home during Toronto rush hour afterwards didn't phase me one bit. When you really want something, there are no obstacles that will slow you down. When I arrived for my appointment I was surprised to see the amount of trees surrounding his property. I envisioned a Toronto home to be barren of any nature and overwhelmed by noise, yet his home was protected by mature greenery and surrounded in quiet. In the big city of Toronto this was like a little pocket of heaven. I felt like my session had already started and I hadn't even met the man.

I entered his home through this beautiful green door, and immediately smelt the aroma of lemongrass. It's not something that everyone uses in their home, and its health benefits are highly sought after by people looking to support an anti-inflammatory diet or seeking digestive support. He was walking the walk of a practitioner, and actually doing the things that he knows are beneficial. He invited me into our session space, and I knew I was exactly where I needed to be. He had a wall of certificates and accomplishments, but he drove home the point that Polarity was the bread and butter of them all. While many other certifications were focused on just the physical body, Polarity focused on the root cause and underlying energy disruption. We spoke about Polarity as well as fascia tissue and its complexity. Throughout my session he educated me on my own body, and asked me to notice if I could sense the subtlety of my fascia tissues moving. He didn't just adjust my body, he brought my own participation into the session by drawing my attention into my body. He told me about his journey of getting to Polarity and having learnt it in the USA. I felt slightly discouraged because if I wanted to be a practitioner of this modality one day I didn't want to have to go to the States.

He shared with me that there was a teacher just a little further north from him who taught classes. He continued to share his wealth of knowledge with me, even giving me an extra anatomy and physiology textbook for my new interests, and provided me with the details for the teacher, Sher Smith. Hopefully she would have an introduction course that I could attend. I reflected on the session the entire drive home. The long drive felt like a blessing giving me time to absorb everything I had learned and experienced.

I felt an ease within my lower back after my session. I didn't know what he did exactly, but something reduced tension in my lower back and my hips. If you've ever felt relief in muscles that have been tense for months or even years then you know what I mean. That alone was enough for me. One session and I was convinced that this was right up my alley, and I needed to know more. I immediately emailed Sher to see if she had any introductory courses coming up. She did. I was signed up within hours of returning home from the day trip to Toronto. I had a sense that Polarity was going to be something monumental in my life and my quick decisions and actions really showed me that. There was no question that this was going to be a huge part of my life, spiritually and otherwise.

As the days, and hours dwindled down for the night before the intro class I felt this ease surrounding me. I didn't feel nervous for the course like I had for many of the previous workshops I had attended. This felt like a natural progression. Effortless, and unforced.

My thin yellow workbook from my Polarity introduction course is never far from me. Not only is it a reminder of where my love for holistics started, it's also filled with a wealth of knowledge of Polarity Therapy and its principles. For an introductory class, I got so much out of it. With Ayurveda laying the foundation of the modality, I was reconnected to nature in a way I never knew I needed. Ayurveda is an ancient, holistic system of healing that sees health as a dynamic balance between body, mind, spirit, and the environment. It teaches us how to live in harmony with nature. The elements of nature—fire, water, air, earth, ether—are present within every aspect of your life. From the powerful way that you walk and manner in which you talk, to the very way you construct your lifestyle and regulate your emotions. It took my spiritual practice to an entirely different level, and provided a new place of awareness to reflect from. I began to look at all aspects of my spiritual practice from journaling to meditation and wonder which element I was, or wasn't, working with.

After the introductory class with Sher I felt as if my eyes adjusted to seeing life in a new way and I could see nature and its elements everywhere and in everything. The course provided theories as to why we might be drawn to more light foods when we're feeling a heaviness in our bodies. The more I thought about it the more I wondered if this could be our intuition, the Seeker within, guiding us toward lighter foods (air) to balance a heaviness (earth) in our bodies, for example. The course taught how our tissues hold energy and how they aren't just tense from being overworked; there may be something deeper within ready to be discovered and released. Connecting my spirituality to my physicality, bringing a holistic and nature-focused perspective into my life, was so expansive and healing for me. I was no longer connecting to nature through childhood memories of running wild on our property or through marathon training runs—I started to connect to it again as if it existed within everything that I did.

Through the holistic approach of Polarity, I discovered something that would support my spiritual journey on a deeper level and become something that allowed me to see others through a new lens. As the Seeker always reminds us, when the student is ready the teacher appears. I was ready for something new in my life, and not only did Polarity become the source of my new interest and education, it also provided a reprieve from the weight of the grief the people around me were feeling and uncertainty in the future of my relationship.

Polarity Therapy is a lifelong study, and I knew in my heart that it would be a part of my life until my final days. After the introduction class, there were further levels that I could complete. The additional hours provided in-depth knowledge of Polarity, Ayurveda and its traditional system of medicine, anatomy and physiology, reflexology, cranial sacral practices, and practical bodywork sequences working with tissue and fascia. All of which assisted in the free flow of energy within the body.

Ten years later and Polarity still fascinates me. I'm always surprised when I re-read a passage that feels as if I've just read it for the first time. I believe moments like that show growth. Who I was when I first read it has grown into someone new, who relates to the text differently, or understands it better than I did the first time.

In the hump, when I was wondering what was next for me and being met with uncertainty in my life, I stayed open. I stayed open to the possibilities of something new. I persevered through the unknowing and discovered not only a new interest, but an entirely new way of working with life, which ultimately led me to deeper self reflection and personal freedom.

Chapter Twelve

CEASE AND DESIST

I woke up one early morning in March 2016. I felt the need to see the sunrise. I found my way down the Niagara parkway, driving past bare vineyards and ended up near the famous Niagara Falls. Close by exists a small place called Dufferin Islands. Think Central Park but in Niagara, ON. I had only been there once before to see a Christmas light show but that morning I was instead watching the sunrise from a bench at the edge of the pond. It was a still morning—nothing moved, not the air, not the water. It was just me and the ducks.

I was internally wrestling with something that I was trying to come to terms with. I had been pretending it wasn't there, distracting myself from dealing with it at every turn, and taking on the weight of responsibility to figure it out all on my own. I began to accept that beneath my desire to maintain and re-energize the relationships in my life, that I actually had begun to subtly try and control them.

Behind every new attempt at connection was me trying to force one. With every new red flag was me justifying it and turning it into a delusion of green rather than seeing it for what it was. I started to feel like Lennie in John Steinbeck's beloved tale *Of Mice and Men.* I felt like I would unknowingly and without ill intention, hold so tightly something I had such affection for that the life would slowly fade from what I was trying to love and nurture. It was a confronting realization, to say the very least.

There was one thing I had that Lennie didn't, though, and that was wherewithal of emotional and self-awareness. I had the opportunity to see how tightly I was holding onto things in my life and make a change. My white-knuckled grip wasn't helping to keep things together. I could see that now, so I knew it was time to let go. Sometimes we can become controlling or even manipulative in defiance of acceptance or surrender. As a competitive person I hated losing, and somehow admitting defeat, or accepting my circumstance, felt like the final buzzer in a game I could no longer play in.

It was that early morning where I discovered that I had inadvertently created a verb for what I had been doing. I "Stacified" things, meaning I always tried to fix it, manage it, or lead it. I would use every tool in my arsenal to try and overcome dysfunction in my friendships and relationships, or help people overcome their own barriers without them asking for my help. It would show up in the most subtle ways, and always with good intentions. But, in the end I realized I was meddling in other people's business. I'd "Stacify" and at the same time take away someone's moment to learn on their own and listen to their inner voice.

"The road to hell is paved by good intentions" became a quote that I finally understood. My ego's desire to help may have actually kept myself or others stuck in what they were ready to let go of. It was a humbling moment in my spiritual journey when I realized that my spiritual voice was not everyone else's. The Seeker within me was designed for only me, just as yours is designed specifically for you.

That morning on the park bench in the stillness with the ducks I made a decision. I realized that the life I was living was no longer sustainable or healthy for me. I came to the understanding that I am not everyone else's inner voice because trying to be left me feeling exhausted, resentful, and bitter. I had a reckoning within myself that quiet morning. In trying to support or lead, I subtly and unintentionally manipulated my surroundings. It wasn't part of my basic human nature but something I learned in order to survive—a shadow I grew many years ago.

At first I felt shame. In a small way I was making it all about me. I judged myself, saying things like: not very aware of you, or that's not very spiritual. Every time I got involved in someone else's life, offered spiritual guidance when not asked, or tried to control the relationships in my life, it was really about me. Again, it wasn't my intention. All I wanted to do was to lift others up, help them overcome what was holding them back, and to discover what existed beneath their own masks. I also was trying to calm what I perceived as the dysfunction around me, and I took it upon myself to fix what I felt needed fixing. This need to fix everything around me was a pattern repeating itself from my childhood and many years after. But, it was time to break the pattern and choose something else. That's awareness after all, bringing something to the conscious mind that was living in the subconscious. This new shift in my perspective of how I saw myself and interacted in my life and the lives of others was playing out in real time on this little park bench.

The decision to constantly step in and help was really showcasing how I felt about myself and others. It would happen so quickly, as if by a muscle reflex of the mind, whenever I'd witness what I perceived was suffering or pain. How often do we jump into action of helping others who have everything available to be able to help themselves? How often do we try to take on the work of their spiritual path when we have a load of our own that requires focus?

Many people who identify as being empathic, spiritual, encouragers, leaders, or dreamers naturally assume these "helping" states with people around them. We want to help, we see their potential or struggle. The big kicker is that unless they approach you for help, they aren't asking you for it. Staying out of it until they ask for help may be the lesson for you to learn like it was for me. Maybe staying out of it and focusing on your own lane—showing proof of your efforts—is the only way for others to see the possibilities and be inspired to take their own steps forward into new potential.

I made a declaration to myself before I left the Dufferin Islands that day. I had done the best I could, but it was no longer what was the best for me, and arguably, maybe not even best for the people around me. My focus now was to stay in my own lane and nurture my own Seeker and inner voice. I declared that I would release any meddling I was doing and leave it to those involved directly. One by one I pulled my focus back to what I needed now and what the Seeker within me was ready to unfold as our next step.

This declaration brought up a few questions: Where am I giving everything I have and leaving myself feeling empty? What is it that I need? What am I ready to focus on within myself? These questions felt huge at the time. To pull my energy and focus back toward myself, when I'd been living externally-focused for so long, was at once refreshing and terrifying. I could have stayed on that island for days, yet knew I needed to eventually go home to settle into this new perspective and way of looking at things.

I never experienced an internal perspective shift like this before in my life. I felt like I had been *(lovingly??)* called out by the Universe. It was powerful in how it changed the way I saw myself and how I interacted with the people around me. When I left the house that morning I didn't expect to be coming home as a changed person.

These awakening moments happen at the most spontaneous times and are unforced. These moments all have something in common for me: I was listening to an internal voice. That voice that asked to go watch the sunrise. There was no immediate destination in mind. Just the desire to see where it leads. It led me to nature, which is unsurprising considering my affinity for heading there whenever I had something going on in my life. From sneaking off to the woods on my childhood home, to walking trails in Niagara, to that very morning on the bench watching the sunrise, being in nature is always where I can see myself and my life more clearly. I began to listen to those moments more and more because in them was always wisdom waiting for me to discover. The Seeker within me always led me to new insights when I didn't fight it but flowed with it instead.

Unconsciously and without intention, we tend to muddle up our lives. Our unconscious patterns and beliefs dictate our choices, and those choices will show in real time. If it's a choice that we make in the betterment of our lives, or a choice we make to feel safe, accepted, or loved, we'll soon see the results of that. Living from unconscious patterns means that we will consistently find ourselves in similar situations and repeatedly play out themes in our lives. Maybe it's a relationship that you've entered because you're scared to be alone, even though there may be no real intimacy or connection. Perhaps it's finding a job that's devoid of fulfillment but you accept because it pays the bills. Do you ever look at your life and wonder what decision you've made that has gotten you to where you are? I spent months on these questions once I looked around and saw what my life had really become.

This moment on the island was the first moment that I truly understood what it meant to surrender to something. There had been glimpses of it in my past but I didn't have a name for it. I would fight tooth and nail for something, showcasing how competitive I was within myself along the way. I thought that never giving up was always a good thing I prided myself in being steadfast, reliable, consistent. But, sometimes you need to surrender the values that you built over a lifetime to maintain a mask or to come back into a balance within yourself. To survive this phase of my life, I needed to cut the emotional weight I was carrying for everyone so that I wouldn't sink to the bottom of my own life.

Over and over again these moments of surrender and deep reflection would come up for me whenever I would notice my innate desire to fix everything around me. Within my fixing, lives over-giving, over-trying, and eventually I am left with everything feeling overwhelming. But it has taken the work of years to notice when I am falling back into this pattern and to pull myself back from it.

You will come to see your own repeated patterns and learn how to disrupt them. Mine, like I said, is a well-intentioned ego-driven desire to fix everything around me leading me to carry more than what is mine. My learned pattern is now to notice, reflect, surrender, and release. Each time you find the courage to let go whatever burdens and patterns you carry, you get to increase your resiliency and trust in your intuition. It's forged and made strong in these challenging moments, and your ability to notice when it's no longer working comes quicker each time. Saying goodbye, letting go, has never come easily for me. It brings forward my abandonment wounding. I have learned through the years that surrendering and letting go, while difficult, is where the healing and evolution happens.

This will be the same for you. So when you have your own moments where things are shifting, like my morning on the bench, know that even though the shift may be challenging and requires perhaps more than you think you can handle, what is on the other side of the shift is more. More of yourself. More trust. More guidance from your Seeker. More connection to your intuition.

The "more" on the other side allows your intuition to become more recognizable. You'll begin to sense things more clearly and quickly in your body. You'll learn what a yes feels like, and you'll learn what a no feels like. As a self-proclaimed habitual over-giver, learning the no was especially important. Learning where a "no" lived in my body has been wonderful. And beyond that, coming more in-tune with my intuition has helped me tremendously along my spiritual journey. We have all been faced with moments when our intuition is practically yelling at us, but if we continue to ignore it, we'll never learn to trust it.

Start small in befriending your intuition and learning to trust it. Starting small could be the decisions around your food choices or lifestyle habits. You don't immediately need to jump into the bigger parts of your life. Get curious and start with fundamentally small questions and notice the response from your body. Notice what comes from your gut or where you feel the answer in your body. Like any good coach told me in my sports days, "Always go back to fundamentals."

We can argue that most relationships with deep meaning and love survive because of the bond of trust. The relationship has been nurtured and respected. The trust that exists makes things easier and life, in turn, feels more effortless with those relationships. The relationship with yourself needs that same respect, nurturing, care, and love. A trust between all the parts of yourself, your Seeker within, and your intuition needs to be built, and even tested, over time. We build trust and bonds with others and rarely focus on the self trust and bonds that we have within ourselves. Beginning to build a relationship with yourself is the keystone to listening to and trusting your intuition and cultivating the courage you need to take action. Through practice and repetition you build on the ability to hear your inner voice more clearly and identify what is ready to be discovered in your life more quickly.

During my Polarity studies we would utilize a sway method to assist in tapping into our internal guidance. It's simple, it's subtle, and for me it's accuracy is undefeated. I first would get grounded and quiet, tuning into my breath. I would ask my body to sway in the direction of yes, almost always for me yes is a subtle sway forward, with no being a subtle sway backwards.

I loved this technique because I could use it anywhere. It was another internal tool that I could take with me and use at any time. I've used it in grocery stores, I've used it in helping to decide holiday purchases, and I've used it in social situations where my intuition was asking me to take notice of something. The sway is so subtle that people around you wouldn't even know it's happening. I would stand feeling connected and self assured with my inner guidance leading me and feeling present in the moment. It's gotten me out of potentially dangerous situations, and it's also helped me identify if a limiting belief was at play in a recent decision making process. "Is this decision or thought motivated by unworthiness?" A sway test would help me continue to learn and go deeper.

Say we don't listen to the call, ignore the signs, or say yes when we sway towards no. What happens when we ignore and disconnect from our intuition, or allow fear or uncertainty to be our guide versus trust and intuition? In my experience when I've said yes to a no moment I feel it immediately in my stomach as if I've been punched in the gut. My intuition had been standing there loud and proud, and my response was to act as if it didn't exist.

But I'll leave these questions here for you to think about:

What could happen when we follow fear, betray ourselves and intuition, and continuously say yes to your no?

What's the price that we pay when we find ourselves in misalignment?

What would be possible if we let go of the self imposed responsibility of holding up the emotional load on our own and we began to live for ourselves?

Chapter Thirteen

THE ME I DIDN'T SEE COMING

As a young woman growing up there was always this expectation and want of marriage and a family. I had checked all the boxes of achievements and did all the right things. When I found myself creeping in on thirty, childless, and in an eight-year relationship devoid of commitment, I felt exhausted of both energy and options. I asked myself: If I'm not going to be a wife or a mother, then who am I? In that moment, it felt like life itself responded saying, "That's a great question, Stacy. Let's find out shall we?" I had done everything "right," but was left with an ache inside and a yearning for more. I was starting to become so resentful about aspects of my life and unable to recognize who I was. My positivity was draining, I barely wanted to leave my house, and my friends and family became worried for my psychological well-being. "You've lost your spark," they would say.

This existential question of who I am, would become a momentous and explosive moment in my life, one where a larger vision for myself would begin to show up. And there was not a thing I wanted to do to stop it. From the morning of inner reckonings on the bench at Dufferin Islands to Polarity crossing my path, I felt as if I was walking in a new and invigorating direction in my life.

Within the months of becoming aware of Polarity Therapy, and making the decision to go for the introduction course, I knew I was learning exactly what the Seeker within me had guided me towards. For the first time in my life I felt inspired and hungry for more education. I dropped out of my head and back into my body. This was the first time I had felt stillness in years. I basked in this feeling and desperately wanted to continue growing my knowledge in the subject.

Nothing can explain the feeling I would get as I would walk into my Polarity classes on the weekends. They were held in a historic red brick building north of Toronto surrounded by trees and wildlife. In the mornings I'd say hello to the same eagle that sat on the same large tree the weekend before, and go into class. Every time I passed through those doors it felt like I was coming home. Something about being at the table with like minded people felt surreal, but I welcomed that feeling with an open heart. I had become accustomed to being the one person in my circles who shared "woo woo" ideas, feeling alien in my own world, but here, I wasn't alone. I felt like I was truly speaking the language of my soul and Seeker for the first time by people who could understand me. Our conversations would often leave me speechless and I would quickly write down the author of the books everyone was sharing. I felt accepted and safe there and it's where I learnt how important it is to be present in your life with yourself and others.

I discovered that there was a sensitivity to me that was honoured in that room. Growing up and throughout my adult life people would tell me to stop being so sensitive, but here, in this space, my sensitivity was my superpower. My sensitivities picked up on the subtle energetic nudges a classmate's body shared with me, and my intuition guided me to where they needed bodywork. It was here where I felt that honesty, trust, and integrity were deeply cherished. These would be traits that would become my new core values, and as I discovered them for myself, I continued to gain clarity in who I was becoming, how I would live, and how I wanted to feel in my life moving forward. This is when I felt alignment for the very first time. Once you feel true alignment, you never forget. You also start to notice everywhere you aren't in alignment.

February of 2018 I honored my own well-being and hit a turning point. I have no intention to romanticize the personal transformation that took place during that time. As I continued to grow in my confidence in my Polarity classes and clinicals, and build myself into the person

I wanted to be in my life, it became clear there was an area within my life that was no longer growing. I deeply wanted to evolve and walk strongly in a new direction, but deep down I felt that I was about to embark on a solitary trip in my life, the Seeker within being my only companion. The masquerade had come to an end for me. My life was changing, I knew it in my core. I just didn't know how much and how drastically things would shift. It was time to let go of the thing that was binding my energy in tightness and restriction.

I was sitting on the couch in my basement with my boyfriend of eight years watching *The Shift* by Wayne Dyer. This was my attempt to infuse Wayne's teachings into my relationship. But there I was again— meddling, acting in stealth, and striking in subtle ways. Falling back into an old habit. I found myself simultaneously watching the movie with him and seeing a clear vision in my imagination of a young girl on a play-ground chasing a little boy and asking him to be her boyfriend. But then she stopped. She stopped chasing the little boy. The little girl realized she no longer needed to chase after anyone—she was no longer begging to be chosen. It made no sense for her to do so. She was wonderful, kind, and caring, all on her own. And I knew when that vision came to me that I was done with trying to make my relationship and life with this man something that it was not. I began to clearly see what had been blurry and hidden from my consciousness for so long. I needed to stand for my worth and believe that I was enough just as I was, and there was no longer a need to go above and beyond just to feel loved or approved of. When I believed that I was enough, I no longer chased, pleaded, or compromised.

I chose myself. I started to feel more at ease and content in my life. I focused on my new passions and no longer found myself aiming to be everything for everyone. I stopped play-acting "the wife" and started pay-ing closer attention to my actions. I stopped trying to control anything, or influence my partner's growth in any way, and stepped back. Peace became more important to me than the potential of what could be.

I saw how quickly things fell away when I stopped trying to keep it all together. Deep down, this was something I was deeply afraid of and part of what took me as long as it did to get to this point. I began to understand what "loving and letting go" really meant and letting myself not be the one to fix it all felt like a huge relief. I felt sad and periodically in disbelief because I knew that we did love each other, but I also knew that the only option to keep it all together was to pretend or continue to sacrifice myself, and that was no longer on the table. That is not love, at least not loving to me. I started to envision what I wanted in a relationship, set the standards that I knew I was worthy of, and began to pay attention to where I was, what I was doing, and how I felt.

I was offered an opportunity to participate in my first firewalk— to experience what it felt like to feel fear and do it anyway. Up until then, it had just been a motto—a simple phrase on the wallpaper of my phone. But this was different. This was a chance to show up for myself, to summon courage from within, and choose to walk forward with my fears. And my biggest fear at the time was ending the relationship and later realizing that it had been a mistake. As I stomped through those hot coals, unscathed and empowered, all the doubt around ending my relationship disappeared.

Four powerful lessons emerged during my firewalk that I still carry with me to this day. Follow your passions. Stay true to yourself. Love yourself unconditionally. Trust that something greater is working with you. That night walking across the coals transformed how I saw myself—both in life and in relationships. In just one evening, I overcame the doubts that were clouding my present and future. I walked through the fire with both fear and courage by my side. Once I fully committed to the decision to let go and choose myself, there was only room for conviction.

I had been reflecting on the areas of my life that were not contributing to my health and happiness—the places out of alignment. The largest and hardest decision was ending the relationship I spent my twenties in, had given all of myself to, and centred my hopes and dreams for a marriage and a family in. We had been through so much together but we were miles apart now. I wanted to be happy, I wanted him to be happy, but we were certainly not the source of this for each other. I was scared, and heartbroken. I knew what was coming, I could feel it.

One divinely chosen night we were reflecting on our relationship in bed together. We thought back to the day eight years prior when we were just friends driving along in his car and first decided to give a relationship a try. "We gave it a good go," was the mutual response, and just like that, in the wake of a long drawn out pause, truth prevailed and we ended it. I didn't know whether to laugh in relief or cry in disappointment as it felt like my life had just, ever so quietly and calmly, blown up. I felt free from the pressure to keep trying to make it work and fit myself into a relationship that I had outgrown. I felt free of the pressure of continued confusion about what to do with my life since the life I planned with my partner was no more. And even though I suddenly didn't know what was up from down, I felt free.

The coming weeks would prove to me how sacred sisterhood is. When I needed support it was my community who were there, and it was them who checked in on me when they knew I was home alone and not doing well. It was them who would bring a smile to my face or just simply sit and be there with me. Show me a woman with a sisterhood and I'll show you a woman who can conquer her despair, who can move out and into a new place, and make it feel like home. I think they actually gave my landlord whiplash with how fast they went to work unpacking!

This would be the first time I would be alone and support myself in eight years. I experienced more grief in the two years that followed than I had in what felt like my entire life. In the void of all uncertainty and sadness I began to feel what I had been repressing. Guilt, shame, resentment, and anger all came to the surface. Thankfully, they were accompanied with hope, compassion, and love. I continued to journal. I started to meditate more consistently and focused solely on my Polarity studies. I swore to myself that I wouldn't fill this new time and space with distractions. I was unwaveringly committed to myself. I continued to learn about energy, and how important it is to move energy through the body, especially our emotions. A decade later, I am still working the repression out of my jaw—when I hold my emotions in, I really hold them in.

This was a new dawn—one where I could feel everything all at once and still move forward. This is where resilience would prove critical. The people in my circles were encouraging me to be gentle with myself during this time, but there was a daring and bold woman ready to live her life. I had been silent about my needs and desires for far too long. I was ready to give myself new experiences that I had only dreamt about, to shake my hips at salsa lessons, and actively pursue my passions and interests without guilt or hesitations.

I would look at the aspects of my personality that had become scared to be seen. In those moments of shying away, quieting down, or closing up, I gave myself full permission to relax and be fully present—with no filter on my words or feelings. I began to no longer hide and inch-by-inch would reclaim my energy, self-esteem, and space as someone that mattered.

When you become more aware of where you want to grow, you also become aware of the traits that are no longer serving you and preventing your growth. This was hard to see because this required me to face and admit to my own toxic traits, and I wasn't always quick to admit when parts of my personality were holding me back. The ego was really good at hiding them and fighting to keep me exactly as I was.

One of my biggest personal lessons was understanding that the most authentic and sustained growth came after ownership. I had to own up and be honest when I wasn't being real. Sometimes I would fall back into old patterns, and in my reflections, I owned it. I practiced living into higher self-esteem and deeper self-confidence. I would think about how I was in salsa class or dancing with friends and vow to stand taller, breathe and smile more, and dance the bachata like I was a pro having fun with everyone else. I loved to dance and declared that I would become so good at salsa I could go to any club and jump right in! I gave myself permission to go out and enjoy life.

I would repeatedly find myself in a new moment where freedom and fear would come knocking. I began to take those micro-moments of fear as an indication that I was ready for the next step. This would often be saying no when others would expect me to say yes, or standing taller with the familiar gusto I had exuded in my barn as a child when I felt myself starting to shrink. It would look like me creating a new boundary and sticking to it even if someone else disagreed with me and the reason why I did it. I would leave feeling shaken and unnerved, but instead of rejecting the opportunity to step into this new me, I would bring up the courage within and face my fears.

I'd ceremoniously thank myself when the uncomfortable stretch of growth was over and take ownership over my timidness and any excuses that came up. I'd have to actively remind myself that every time I faced my fears that I came out on the other side stronger, more self-assured, and more loving to myself and those around me. I also became quicker at seeing what was present in my life, no longer living solely in the future potential of what could be.

My saving grace during this period was my deep conviction to myself, my faith, and the vision that had started to take real form. On the most loneliest nights of my newly single days, I'd often find myself looking around my apartment in a bit of a daze. I think back to my first night in my new place. My friends had all gone home, and the reality of my new life was setting in. I felt anxious and felt unsettled. In the soft glow of my salt lamp, I noticed a chair in the corner of the room—and I felt the presence of Jesus occupying that space. Clear as day, I could see him sitting there. He didn't say anything. He didn't need to. I could feel that he wanted me to know I wasn't alone, and he'd be watching over me through the night, and in the days to come.

While I grew up within the Anglican church, as I got older my attendance would only be consistent around Easter or Christmas. Throughout my adulthood, I gradually distanced myself from organized religion and the church, not due to any negative experiences or familial pressure, but because it simply didn't resonate with my personal truth. Instead, I allowed myself the space to cultivate my own relationship with Jesus, guided by discernment and my own lived experiences.

This relationship continues to evolve and deepen with time. I knew I was being watched over by a friendly presence and that everything was going to be okay. There was a love and respect that had become so present within my life giving me the momentum and fuel for my ambitions and larger vision for myself. While there were moments of self doubt there were also whispers of encouragement. There were days that I didn't listen, and there were days where I allowed the whispers to drown out any self doubt that arose. The days where I made the most strides and transformative growth were also the days where I felt the most unsure. It's not often spoken about how moving through the uncertainties can bring you the most tremendous clarity and comfort on the other side, but it's true.

In daily spiritual practice I would place pen to paper, set a timer for twenty minutes, take a deep breath and write. This was one little step in my spiritual practice that would support me through this period of my life. This became an immovable daily commitment, even just to dump all of my frustrations of the day out on the paper versus on myself or other people. It helped me to ride the emotional waves so that I could come back to centre.

Often, I would learn where my strengths lived and where I was required to build more resources within myself to stoke an inner fire to carry through. Each time I got stronger, I relied less on others, and grew a confidence within myself that I could have my own back and my own heart. I knew that if there were days that I didn't or couldn't have my own back, I would have countless people in my corner who I had met along the way that would be more than happy to answer my message or pick-up the phone. I began to trust that I had created a network around me—one that made living life to the fullest easier, and struggling in my darkness more bearable—reminding me that I was not alone. It would prove to me that if you had days where you felt insignificant that you might be one of the most significant people to someone else.

If there is a way of life you have dreamed for yourself, nurture it in any way you can. Through one choice and one boundary at a time you'll discover more of who you really are, what you really want, who you really want to be, and...who you are not. Look at the areas of your life that are not aligned to who you are, what you want to create, or how you want to feel. Is there one thing that jumps out at you right now that you know is not aligned to your highest good, or that the Seeker within is illuminating for you?

When I look back at how my life was mapped out for me a decade ago—with marriage, children, and a very different career and education path—I wouldn't even recognize that person. I am now a person I never saw coming. So when you sit down and inspirations or dreams come to mind, whether it be mundane or life-changing, pay attention to it and welcome that wonder into your life. It may just be the you that you didn't see coming—yet is already on its way.

Chapter Fourteen

SPIRALING UP

You're sticking the knife in and twisting it." One of my coaches said to me when I decided to move on and let go of my old life. This particular day I was feeling a mix of sadness, regret, and a pull to backtrack my steps. The first step was actually saying that the relationship was over. The second step was actually doing it and sticking with it. I had been spending time looking for a new place, saving up deposits for the first and last months, and coming home nearly every day to an item of mine stacked next to the front door with a statement from my ex saying, "I didn't want you to forget this." It was a punch in the gut every day. I'd walk in the door and make my way to my bedroom, closing the door firmly behind me. "Thanks for helping me move out," I'd mutter to myself with contempt, feeling as if all sense of empathy had evaporated in our connection with one another. This went on for three long months after the decision to go our separate ways was made.

I didn't have my ducks in a row. I wasn't prepared to be apartment hunting so randomly in my life. We had lived in the house together for six years, so long we were common law. But, because it wasn't a matrimonial home, and my name wasn't on the title, I had no claim to it when we broke up. I was really starting over. I hadn't been financially planning for this change in my life. Eventually I found a couple apartments to look at, and I was quickly humbled by how rental rates had risen since my collegiate days.

The longer I stayed in the house, the worse I felt. It wasn't hostile but this is where I learnt that just because something doesn't become explosive doesn't mean it's a healthy way to live. I went from flying high on personal power and newfound freedom to feeling like a squatter in my ex's house, one that I used to consider to be my home and had envisioned my future in. One moment I'd feel elated and the next moment I would feel completely defeated. I needed to get out, and soon. It really was like sticking a knife in myself and twisting it.

I had some pretty solid ideas of what I was looking for in a new place. I wanted something above ground and my own unit, no basement apartments with people above me I could hear walking around late at night or early mornings. I wanted privacy and space, and ultimately I wanted to feel inspired. I wanted to start my new life feeling encouraged to keep going every day, yet here I was still sitting in the remnants of my old life with new boxes stacking up each day. I had a vision, now it was time to go get it.

I made it to my first appointment and after searching the grounds for ten minutes finally found the property manager's office. They showed me one of their four buildings and I immediately knew it was going to be a no for me. I kept on walking and following them anyway. Down to the basement apartment we went. Renovations were currently happening to remove old carpets, but I was confident that nothing could get the smell out of that building. We entered the unit and my heart sank. I asked "When is the unit available?" "Now," the manager replied. I was utterly shocked. This "move in ready" apartment showed no signs of prideful ownership, and just standing in the small living room I felt a wave of discouragement run over me. I wanted to give up on myself completely. I felt resigned from life and utterly defeated.

It was then that my Higher Self swooped down and stood next to me and said, "Are we done here? Can we go look at places we are worthy of?" I could feel and see her, standing to my right. She was a vision of love and hopefulness, healthy and bright, and in that moment I never felt more clear. Suddenly, I believed in myself again, and was reinvigorated with life and the courage to keep going.

I thanked the manager for her time and left. I went back to my car and sat there for what felt like an eternity, just staring out the window feeling slightly hopeless on the apartment front with a playlist of faith artists playing in the background.

I had begun listening to worship music not because I joined a church or committed to religion, but because it nourished a benevolent space within my spirit that had been hit with heartache. It helped revive a lightness in me, and at this time in my life it was deeply needed. I knew I needed to leave my old place, and maybe I was being too picky or optimistic in the current rental environment of Niagara. I had one more place to look at that week so I made the decision to do a little drive by. I knew that if I didn't like it, I wouldn't bother going to view it. I wouldn't repeat what I had just done.

There it was. Beautifully maintained with flower beds and pots, a rose garden and even a fountain. I felt it immediately. This red brick building was going to be my new home—of that I was certain. I sat at the traffic light, right in front of the building and said this is where I'm going to create my new life, and this is where I'm going to help change the lives of other people. I didn't know how I was going to do that, I just knew I would. I drove home and wrote in my journal all the visions of how I would feel in this new place. Knowing the natural light alone would be enough to bring some light back into my own life. I brought every ounce of positivity and gentleness I could muster to my meeting with the owner and he blew me away.

"Home Temples," he called them. A place for people on an awakened path in life to inhabit while they create their new lives. What was this magic? I never heard of a landlord who built accommodations with such an intention, but talk about alignment. I basically threw my first and last month's rent at him, and asked, "Where do I sign?"

I left that meeting and have never felt so grateful while signing my name on a contract. A few short weeks later I moved into the building, and began to settle into my new place. I left my house key in the mailbox of what was my home for the last six years, and as I shut the lid I knew I'd never go back. It was a key to a door I would never open again. I looked around at the gardens we had built and nurtured, and knew I'd never step foot in them again, and I let go of the images flooding my mind of future children in there with me. Something about shutting the lid on the mailbox gave me closure. It didn't come from a conversation with my ex, or the need to say goodbye, it came from an intentional moment, a symbolic moment, of laying down a key to a life I was no longer living, and a life showing no signs it wanted me to stay and help it thrive.

Sometimes the life we think is ahead of us alters its course, and leaves us having to bravely embrace the unknown. Our ability to accept this fact will vary from person to person, and while some may traverse it with ease, some of us seeking a new direction in life may find it a great struggle. Your ability to show compassion for yourself and the people you interact with on your spiritual journey may at times feel like the only thing in your control, so please hold this truth close to your heart.

The upper level, or the "Penthouse Suite" as I would call my new place, increased my desire to attract more abundance into my life. Every morning when I'd wake up I felt free, and was ready for what the days ahead would bring. It wasn't all sunshine and rainbows though. There would be moments when I'd feel the high of living in the unknown and embracing new beginnings, and then the lows of bringing suppressed emotions to the surface. With self reflection comes great awareness, and it's an up and down road.

The Seeker within me rose up asking more questions. I was no longer distracted by relationship woes and hindsight of the past and my relationship dynamic was kicking in full gear. Five years before my relationship ended I knew it was not the right one for me and that it would inevitably come to an end. I disconnected from my discernment, overrode what I knew deep within myself, and caved to my inner desire to be chosen. I had been crying out for his love, continuously giving everything I could to maintain our stalled relationship, leaving me unfulfilled and unheard. This is the result of trying to force something that is out of alignment. It may seemingly work for a while, but it will always come to a head eventually.

How often do we draw out a decision that we know is best for us? In these drag-your-feet moments fear and self doubt can arise. We can find ourselves on a slippery downward trajectory.

During the downward spiral we make excuses or find ways to justi-fy our behaviour or the behaviour of others. We may talk ourselves out of decision making, unconsciously thinking that if we don't make the decision, then the result isn't our fault. Maybe it's the fear of making a mistake or a change, allowing the ego to operate unfettered behind the scenes. While you may find your current state of being or lifestyle un-comfortable, at least it's predictable to you. This is how we keep ourselves stuck and stagnant and re-entering patterns. We get comfortable in un-comfortability and conformity because the unknown is too scary or feels like the choice is too big or Life altering.

When you succumb to your fears and doubts for too long it will begin to feel like potential slipping away, you'll feel the loss of your spark, and will feel uninspired in your life. Rather than break free of the down-ward spiral, shake things up a bit, and set the ego in the backseat, we become accustomed to living in lower energetic frequencies.

When I noticed this downward spiral and lower-frequency living in my life, I began listening to Dr. Joe Dispenza's meditation series called *Tuning Into New Potentials* each day. During the meditation, I would ac-tivate my heart and embrace elevated emotions by bringing my heart and brain into a coherent state to raise my energetic frequency. I'd envision what was available to me in my life, what I could potentially achieve, and build the vision into something that made my heart sing, filling my body with love and gratitude for the future. I'd visualize the possibilities to such detail that they weren't just ideas, but vivid realities I was immersed in.

Whenever I felt I was in a funk, I'd tune in and wouldn't leave my meditation mat until I felt a shift. I no longer wanted to live my life as if feeling uplifted was a fleeting occurrence. I buckled down and chose to feel it intentionally, every single day. In a moment I'd go from sitting mundanely on my mat to feeling euphoric, shivers running up and down my spine, goosebumps appearing on my skin. I would feel such a light-ness within when thinking about looking over the historic ruins of Ma-chu Picchu knowing one day that I would get there, and grateful for the body that would carry me each step of the way to its gates high up in the Andes Mountains.

There's a visual that I would use on a regular basis during my meditation practice and reflection moments. It was created by David R. Hawkins, and it's called, *The Map of Consciousness.* It's a multicoloured chart ranking levels of human consciousness on a logarithmic scale from 0 to 1000, representing a spectrum from low-frequency states like shame and guilt at the bottom of the chart, to high-frequency states like love and peace at the top. When you feel an emotion, the frequency of it vibrates through your body and spirit. Dr. Joe Dispenza speaks to this as well. When we've lived in an energetic state for so long our cells become addicted to being in that energetic state, which is why for some, changing habits can be so difficult. It's not that we can't change our habits, but we need to teach our cells a new way of feeling until the older, lower frequency shifts or those cells are replaced by newer vibrant ones. Until then, the mind and body drive to return to a state of normality, latching on to opportunities that keep us in that old emotional state.

It became a daily mission for me to find a neutral space within myself—or to reach a higher energetic frequency—as outlined in *The Map of Consciousness.* It also served as an important reminder not to match other peoples lower energies in my life. I can witness them where they are at and hold compassion, but my main focus and responsibility became my own energetic state and some days, that felt like a full-time focus.

As I settled into my new home I was feeling very optimistic. Although, some nights, like an energetic whiplash, I'd go from feeling excited for my future to regretting my past decisions. If self doubt came for a visit I could feel the pull further down towards feelings of guilt or even resentment. My daily spiritual practice of meditation and journaling became more than just reflection moments, they became the parts of my day where I could remind myself where I wanted to be in my life and to persevere. If that didn't work, and I found myself laying in bed with no motivation I'd put on *Star Wars: The Force Awakens.* It reminds me that I will always be on the "light side," and will always be a part of The Resistance. When it's over, I get up, open my blinds, put on some music, and start my day anew. Watching this film is my backup plan if my spiritual practice doesn't quite cut it—and it always works for me. Honoring what you need to come out of a funk is an act of self-acceptance—and a quiet rebellion when it feels like outside forces are trying to keep you down.

Without my daily check-ins I would catch myself falling down the slippery slope of doubt and sitting waist deep in blame and inaction. I remember one particular day about a year after I moved. I came home after a rough day at work and I was exhausted.

I was lost in thought while walking from my parking space to the base of the large staircase that led up to my apartment. Playing in my mind was some romcom movie scenario where my ex would be sitting on the steps, asking for us to get back together and make it work. Scenes from movies like the final moment at Seb's jazz club in *La La Land* and the fountain scene at the end of *Someone Great* would have perfectly captured my daydream—my deepest yearning for love fulfilled, without the distractions and complexities of "real" life. I was mentally and emotionally rehearsing the epitome of a love story. But this was no romcom. No one sat on my steps awaiting my arrival. I felt sick to my stomach—maybe from my thoughts, maybe from work. At this point, I couldn't tell. All I knew was: no one was there.

After dinner that evening I began my evening routine. I was on my meditation mat resisting my practice and procrastinating. I was full of thoughts of regret. I began questioning myself: Was this the wrong move? Did I do the right thing? Maybe I had been too critical? I knew that I had said mean things when I was angry and resentful, and maybe that's how we got here. If I helped him more financially maybe it never would have happened, or maybe I nagged him too much for his financial choices. Did I rush something or not try hard enough?

I was doubting myself and my choices, and my energy was in free fall. I felt myself starting to spiral downward—physically tense and nauseous, my body matching the emotional turmoil. In perhaps the least helpful decision I could have made at that moment, I picked up my phone and started to scroll. As I flipped through my Facebook feed, a video appeared—it was a gender reveal party. For my ex. He was having a baby. I had only been gone for just over a year. I was in disbelief. Eight years together—no commitment, no marriage, no baby. The careful and intentional vision I had created for my future—with him and for myself—was now going to belong to someone else.

These are the kind of moments where time seems to stand still. In these moments we have a window of an opportunity to choose our next thoughts and steps purposefully and wisely. This flash of new information had the potential to spiral me down even further and diminish all the work I had done within my spiritual practice. If left unchecked, it could open a door for negative beliefs—or even the feeling of betrayal—to rush in and take over.

When intense emotions are felt, the chemical reaction in the brain flushes the central nervous system. When you feel rage or hurt, a different part of the brain takes over and you can make reactive decisions. It's like an emotional hijacking between the brain and the body, and you can forget all reasoning if your self awareness doesn't drop in first.

I refused to let this video and my response to it emotionally flood me. In these moments, we get to decide whether these external experiences have power over us—or whether we have power over our response to them. I forced myself to see reason and it brought me back to more rational thinking. I knew I had made the right choice. I knew I could trust my intuition. When I checked in with myself, the correctness of my decision to leave the relationship felt true for me. Even though I had a flush of heightened emotion while already starting to spiral downward, I was able to bring myself back and reclaim my personal power. I physically shook it off and was able to refocus. "Okay, moving on!" And move on I did.

I felt like Iris from my favourite movie, *The Holiday*. In this scene Iris is crying over her arrogant ex-situationship with Jasper, breathing in toxic gas from her stove to numb her emotions after finding out some upsetting news. A notification rings from her computer that snaps her out of it. She gives herself a little slap on the face and says, "Low point!... Low point." This felt like that.

The entire day had me teetering on the cusp of a complete shutdown. The beliefs I had in my subconscious had started to return and bubble up from deep within my mind. This experience could have further solidified a belief that I wasn't enough or loveable, but I refused to let it. Through breathwork and self control, the chemical flush within my nervous system dissipated, and I returned to my newer more assured self able to think rationally. I put my phone away and re-focused on my spiritual practice.

I was determined to stay high energetically, not succumb to my past or let my ego pull the strings of my insecurities like a wizard behind a curtain. It became clear that my inner child, who has felt similar pains of feeling unloved, was looking for support. This experience had the potential of sending me spiraling downward into victim or low self worth, but instead I chose to stay in my practice, acknowledge my inner child, and focus on moving forward and spiraling up instead. Because of my choice to spiral upward rather than slip down, I was able to have a good night's sleep and embrace the days ahead with more confidence.

Waves of grief for my old life would swoop in out of the blue. I'd think back about good times, nearly forgetting about the fact that I had gotten to such a place emotionally that one night I said to myself "I'm unloveable." I said it like a fact and had no other emotions behind it I believed deep down on some fundamental level that I was hard to love no matter how hard I loved others. It was the only thing that made sense. It was reminders like this that actually became the signs and fuel I needed to keep myself vibing high. I'd remind myself that I left a life behind where I felt hard to love and unworthy of fighting for, and it snapped me out of any defeating or victim mindset I'd fall into. I began to remember all the red flags I ignored, or all the moments I was home alone unsupported, or asked to sacrifice my peace for the convenience of others, my belongings slowly piling up being ushered out the front door. Just like that, like the snap of my fingers, I was back in growth and self love action.

During my time in Niagara my circle had slowly grown to become one of reliable support and sisterhood. They'd remind me to keep moving, hold my hand when I cried, and encourage the light to return back into my daily life. Their sheer dedication to celebrating my courage to start over fueled my fire to keep going, and would remind me why it's important to let your circles change. I was no longer surrounded by people I didn't trust, who spewed hatred behind my back, and who had no desire to put care and effort into our connection.

I continued to try new things and challenge myself in new ways to keep life exciting and give me something to look forward to. I made plans, and filled my calendar with new experiences and something fun or rejuvenating to do. As I regrew my self esteem I'd find myself slowly starting to feel whole again and not having to work quite so hard to avoid spiraling down. I accepted that it wouldn't be some overnight overhaul, and I trusted that I was learning what I needed to in divine time. I trusted that I was being shown the next step to take by the Seeker within me, never rushing through the teachable and anchoring moments that were helping me grow each day. Do not rush this process. Try to anchor in the new you as you work through it.

I was reading back through my journal entry one day. I found a section I wrote about how I wanted to feel in my new place. And there I was, sitting on my yoga mat in the middle of my new apartment feeling everything I'd written, and more. It was better than I could have imagined. How can you not feel gratitude for that?

We have to be patient with the process of spiraling upward. The discovery of emotions and beliefs can run deep and be layered beneath one another, sometimes so much so that you don't even know they're there. One moment you may feel low, but with dedication to your spiritual practice, you can find yourself rising right back up again.

My own journey has been a testament to this. Little did I know that when I sat in front of the apartment building, quietly telling myself I was going to change lives in my new "home temple," I was setting the stage for what was to come. Shortly after moving in, I started my business, Elevation Coaching. Over the years ahead, I had the privilege of supporting others in finding self love, offering spiritual guidance, and creating a Polarity Therapy wellness program for kids—one of the first of its kind in the Niagara region, and perhaps even in all of Canada. Without realizing it, every pivot, class, and moment of inspiration gently led to the creation of something new and meaningful.

Begin your self discoveries with compassion and an open mind. Let yourself grieve connections with people and unfulfilled old dreams and move on. If you find yourself falling down a slippery slope, practice tapping into new possibilities, not succumb to the deeply ingrained beliefs or fears pulling you further down. Most of them aren't even true, it's just some ego trying to keep you safe and unchanged. When intense emotions arise, notice the chemical flush moving through your body, and allow yourself to ride it like a wave. In most cases, it subsides within ninety seconds, and within that very sacred amount of time, you can do a lot of beneficial internal work leading to deep, lasting transformation. Tap into your inner resilience, buckle down and do the hard work, bring yourself back up again, and go live your life. You may be surprised by what life has in store as a result.

Chapter Fifteen

BELIEVE IT OR NOT

He was on my small computer screen but he felt larger than life. He was dressed casually with a ball cap and his deep voice felt as if radiated from his feet and projected across the auditorium. He was a presence on stage, and I was captivated by every word. I was early in my journey of answering the Seekers' questions of why we put ourselves in situations, or why we live in limitations, and it led me to one of my new teachers, Tony Robbins. His teachings, along with my fascination with Joe Dispenza's work, created an unmatched acceleration in my growth and the relationship I have with myself.

Their paralleled teachings about the subconscious mind and its power in controlling our lives had me hooked. I began to notice when my current behaviours and way of thinking was being challenged. I'd feel unsettled emotionally, and knew that deep within my subconscious an old script was playing out. These were stories the ego labeled as beliefs about myself or things I was told to do or say. When I would notice this, it felt like the Seeker within was calling me out—not to shame me, but to call me forward into a higher potential. I often found myself asking: Why did I just do that? Where did that thought come from? Why did I allow that to happen? Asking these deeper questions is the first step to awareness, and awareness is the first step to change.

The ability to hold deep rooted beliefs and fears is the power of the subconscious mind. Within it exists a complex webbing of choices and beliefs made over time. Those choices and beliefs build upon each other creating a personality that makes us who we are. It's the birthplace of our insecurity and confidence, and the keystone to true and lasting transformation. The subconscious mind is this silent powerhouse in our lives that remembers absolutely everything. Every conversation, every hurt, every trauma, and every inspiration are captured here. It remembers the exact moment you made a decision—big or small—that shaped who you believed yourself to be, or what you believed others thought about you. It remembers every negative idea you believed about yourself even if you eventually forget over time. The conscious mind may have forgotten, but the subconscious sure hasn't. The subconscious mind is where the ego has unpacked its bags, is living rent free, and has brought with it every single item it has collected over the years.

A major chunk of the work I needed to do was distinguishing if a thought about myself or others was a belief that limited me in my growth or a belief that I would continue to nurture and carry forward with me in my life. From the bathtub that evening believing I must be unlovable to showing myself love and knowing I was worthy, took a lot of time and practice and continues to this day.

I often reflect back to the young girl that I was when I started to feel that I wasn't enough. Was it back when my dad started to feel distant, or when, as a C student, I was being compared to my academic A plus sister? Was it my parents divorce, and my struggle to fit in socially? Was it that I never physically felt desirable or represented the perfect body? Was it cancelling my plans to fit into someone else's, or feeling emotionally drained in all my relationships? My choices were making a statement about how I felt about myself. In all of these instances, I believed I wasn't important enough, valuable enough, worthy enough. Never enough. I believed I wasn't enough. Period.

The power of the subconscious mind is where habitual thinking and recurring patterns eventually dictate what we believe about ourselves and others, and further influence the choices and subsequent actions that make up our lives. I had years of experiences that led me to feel that I wasn't enough, and it took me a while to finally see the deeply ingrained beliefs that were driving my actions, thoughts, or words. Like a well worn bad habit we can create beliefs about ourselves that aren't true, and in doing so, invite an energy into our life of victimization or oppression.

You don't know what you don't know. This is why it's imperative that you lead with compassion and forgiveness as you walk a spiritual path. You must decide to openly, and without judgement, look upon all areas you discover about yourself, the good, the bad, the not-so-great. All the parts of you were created with the knowledge and information you had at the time. So, as you grow and evolve personally and spiritually, your thoughts, beliefs, and patterns need to be questioned against your new knowledge and information. Now that you know the power of your thoughts, you get to choose which ones you latch onto and believe, and which ones require a reframing in the way you look at things.

It is here that you may become overwhelmed or judgemental of yourself because of all the years you didn't know what you know now. You may struggle to accept yourself for who you were, the choices you made, and the life you lived. You may also find yourself grieving the version of you that never was, feeling as if you weren't given a fair start right out of the gate. But, the past is gone. You did the absolute best you could with the knowledge and information you had at the time. What matters is what we decide today. Now that you know, what will you decide? What will you believe about yourself? What kind of life will you choose to live?

The beliefs that are hidden deep within the mind and have gone unnoticed most of your life will become the shadow work part of your journey. Unearthing those may even become your own "Dark Night of the Soul" path as uncovering one belief only then shows another. Grace, forgiveness, and self compassion will guide your way through the shadow parts of yourself. That, and your spiritual practice will help support you every step of the way. It will be through the uncovering of what has gone unseen for years that will allow you to really start to supercharge your spiritual journey and see just how powerful you are.

Dr. Joe Dispenza is often quoted: Change your thoughts, change your life. This is echoed by Dr. Wayne Dyer and many other teachers in this world. They understand the power of the subconscious mind and how the beliefs we have within ourselves drive decision making and the way that we view the world around us. These beliefs are like invisible lenses—glasses you don't even realize you're wearing—that filter the world you take in through our senses. They're shaped by the beliefs held in your subconscious mind, which ultimately form your individual reality. If the way we think causes specific emotions, and those emotions produce specific chemicals and energetic frequencies that run through our central nervous system, then all day long the subconscious mind is dictating the way we view life, state of our cells, and the health of our body.

Like an eager Canadian beaver I wanted to get to the bottom of every single limitation that exists within my subconscious mind. I would dig and dig, over-analyzing every single action or thought that I had. I realized quickly that this was not sustainable nor the path that I wanted to take for myself. I would come across others in spiritual communities that seemed almost as if they were lost within the fractals of their subconscious mind. They reminded me of a gold miner who had fallen into hysteria in search of the gold nugget that would change their lives, getting sucked into the promise of the next big discovery. I didn't want to be a fractaled version of myself burning out along the way, and the Seeker within me didn't either.

What's meant to be discovered will be—without force, without obsessing over it. What's meant to show itself to you now will do so. Even still, I'd feel like a break was required after giving so much focus to my subconscious, so I'd head to the movies or sit on a beach to take in the view, or enjoy a sunset chat with a friend. I just needed a break from it all sometimes. After all, if I was doing the work to change my thinking, then my brain was changing its chemistry and I needed to allow it the time to do so.

It's around this time that I was going deep into my subconscious when I learned that I needed to stay in my own lane of healing and not fall into what others were doing and how they felt healing should be done. I'd been encouraged by a friend to give psilocybin a try. They swore by it but my discernment helped me check in with myself before simply following their lead. I eventually chose not to because even though it worked wonders for them and they felt great using it, it didn't feel right for me at the time. My initial gut reaction steered me away. I gave myself permission to heal in the ways that felt like the right fit for me and trusted myself enough to know what I would need next and act on it at the right time. It wouldn't be until 2021 that the right time presented itself, and it was a beautiful experience that I hold dear to this day.

I attended a workshop in the greater Toronto area by a man named Dr. Shad Helmstetter. His focus is on neuroplasticity and using self talk to reprogram the mind. I became curious about the way I spoke to myself. It was mostly the moments where I felt emotionally activated on some level that the self talk became loud and clear, and not in a supportive or loving way. My Polarity studies taught me the power of noticing, and becoming aware of something before applying judgments. The noticing of self-talk paired together so well with what Polarity was teaching me that it quickly became a new focus area for me. I wanted to see what I was saying to myself when I wasn't in those charged moments and my voice was unkindly screaming at me. What was the running script that was determining my self-perception and how I moved about the world? Once I started to notice that, my curiosity led me to look at how that script had been dictating my life. It was a humbling discovery, to say the very least.

I started to discover that some beliefs that I held had been created back in childhood and adolescence, creating the initial subconscious script. They were then reaffirmed in my teenage years, giving more prominence to the script. By then, the running dialogue in my mind was well established and brought into adulthood, leading me in directions that would validate what I was subconsciously telling myself for years. Without noticing, my self-perception became more and more solidified and would run amok on my subconscious mind. Each time a cancelled weekend with my dad or a long-term relationship came to an end, I firmly believed that I was unlovable and unimportant. But it wasn't until that night in the bathtub where the inner belief came forward, planting its flag and saying it out loud, "I am unlovable," that I was able to look at that inner belief head on. Truth is, sometimes plans change or relationships run their cycle and there is no big story or belief that needs to be assigned to it. Without the subconscious belief that I was unlovable and unimportant, the situation with my dad and my previous relationships, for example, wouldn't have felt so devastating. But because I didn't know that I was believing that about myself based on a script that started to be written in my childhood, I assigned a story to these situations. I couldn't see that plans changed or relationships had run their course; I saw it as a flaw within myself. A flaw that validated my inner, subconscious belief.

Beliefs like "I'm unloveable" or "I'm not good enough" are what's called a limiting belief and they feed a further dysfunction beneath it. It creates its own slippery slope where you then accept situations and experiences that validate or re-affirm that belief. The ego doesn't want change, remember, and changing the script isn't something that it wants. These limiting beliefs are like an open wound to the ego. Raw, unhealed, and being fiercely protected. So you will be put in situations and be surrounded by people who affirm your self-perception. This will continue until you have your very own "bathtub" moment when the belief either forces itself to the surface or you go looking for it. I have had both happen, as I am sure you will too.

The linchpin in your healing process, and something the Seeker is eager for you to discover, is realizing that you are the one keeping the script running. Ownership has always been the most polarizing conversation in healing. When we take ownership we can't blame, and many of us love to blame who we are on other people. Have you ever thought that you acted a certain way because of something someone else said or did? Or, have you ever believed that you are the way that you are because of what was done to you in the past?

You can blame things outside of yourself and build yourself a home in victimhood, or you can decide to work with your subconscious mind and transform the beliefs that you hold about yourself. There is no right or wrong in choosing either path. Everyone has the right to choose. For you and I, though, we have chosen the route of ownership and accountability. This means that we have to be cautious and diligent in paying attention to the thoughts running through our minds, both in moments of high emotional charge and in quiet moments when we're calm and with ourselves. We have chosen to rewrite the script, and that takes work.

Take an example of two people born into poverty. One grows up believing and telling themselves that they are poor and always have been. All they know is not having enough money, or barely getting by, and each overdraft or final notice would reinforce that belief. The other, made choices to create financial wealth, to save and learn how to invest, telling themselves that they would never live in poverty again, reinforcing a belief in the subconscious that they were on their way to financial freedom. Both were born into similar circumstances, but the first fell victim to what they knew and never took on the work to further understand finances, the latter grew their knowledge and understanding and took matters into their own hands breaking free of their circumstances.

Dr. Joe speaks to it often. You are either living your life towards a future self and the possibility of who you can be, or you are living in the past keeping yourself stuck. Every moment of new awareness grants you an opportunity to choose how you live. When you believe that you are worthy, and when you believe that you are loved and supported, you get to choose what's next. You are not beholden to someone else's ideas about you or the limiting beliefs that you have accepted about yourself.

The choice to move forward starts and ends with you, and now, you are aware of it. There are no more classes, no more teachers, and no more mentors who will come and say this to you as if it's the first time. Now you know. As the masquerade continues to end and you discover the bonds that hold you in your past, it's up to you to transform your beliefs and rise above them. It's up to you now to discover the beliefs that exist within your subconscious mind, and to work with the Seeker within to discover what they are. Trust that all will be revealed in time as long as you are willing to pay attention, and notice within your body when the time comes for you to put the work in and discover what's trying to speak to you from your subconscious mind—and when it's time to have a break.

If you look around you, at your circles and your daily interactions, there are signs everywhere of what you've created up until now. Perhaps you can look around and feel profound gratitude for the life you've created for yourself and the people around you. On the other hand, you might recognize that old patterns and habits have been running wild, unchecked for decades, and you're now ready to transform your life.

Thoughts like "I always have the worst luck" or "I'm never enough" are not permanent. They can be rewritten over time by flipping the scripts you tell yourself and detaching that vocabulary from who you are. Whatever you believe about yourself to be true, you will find things in your life to affirm these beliefs. What you see, how you feel, and the stories you tell yourself are powerful. So make sure they're ones you want to affirm in your life.

You may find that as your beliefs about yourself shift, your life takes on a whole new meaning. You may find less stress or that your circles begin to shrink, that the phone quiets down and that you crave solitude a little more. You may feel disconnected from your job and want to follow a different path. Honour your experience, grieve what has been lost or changed, and let go. Find peace and move forward.

Chapter Sixteen

PATHS, PALACES, AND PERSPECTIVE

A nd now it's time to lay back into Shavasana." A four syllable word never sounded so sweet, and for those who've been through a yoga session know it symbolizes that your session is coming to an end. It also means being able to lie back and let the weight of the world come off your shoulders. Shavasana for me became the moment where I let the power of the planet do all the work and I got to let go, surrender to the moment, and just be free to exist without agenda.

Yoga became a part of my weekly routine. A friend of mine who was my Polarity homework guinea pig began teaching yoga. Her weekly classes quickly became a top priority for me. Yoga gave me the solace to drop into my body and out of my head, similar to how I would feel during my own Polarity sessions. They both reminded me how supported we are by nature, how powerful our breath is, and how energy needs our help to facilitate its movement throughout our bodies. Without us energy can get stagnant, but with our help we can create a free flow of energy through our bodies. We have to show up for ourselves, the body cannot do it all on its own.

My love for nature came back online during this time in my life. I knew that I may never again see the woods from my blissful childhood days, but it didn't mean that nature wasn't available to me or that there weren't other woodlands ready for exploration. In Niagara there's a collection of trails called Short Hills Provincial Park. By car it was just five minutes up the road or twenty minutes by bike. With my dog Mercedes gone now, I'd often hit the trails alone, just me and my favourite hiking stick. "Just bring a stick with you" still echoing in my mind. I'd pull into the gravel parking lot off Pelham Road and its surrounding vineyards. Every week the vineyards would change appearance looking full and smelling more fragrant as the season progressed. You could always tell when harvest season was coming. The grapes smell on the verge of bursting, and going past the vineyards is a gift to the senses. This was far different from the duck blind, forest, and cattails I was used to and I can't say that I minded. Before I'd even started my hike, the smell from the vineyard would help me stay present and able to appreciate the beauty all around me.

Nature quickly became my therapy as I settled into my new apartment and life. I was living in the unknown of post breakup wonders, and nature sure made it a more enjoyable and peaceful transition. In the evenings I'd do yoga or stretch outside by the fountain, and the weekends were spent hitting the trails. The movement was pivotal to keeping my energy up and processing emotions that I'd suppressed for years. I was no longer a runner, but enjoyed a peaceful time outside. In the hour and half hike through the hills I found peace and quiet again. I found quiet from my thoughts, from my fears, and from over-analyzing what my life had become. For that hour and half I got to turn off my mental gymnastics and simply muscle my way through the hills and trails. I'd stop when I'd notice a berry bush and let myself, and the inner child, pluck a fresh berry and savour its sweetness. There was nothing for me to do but put one foot in front of the other. In the forest I felt like I could breathe again. When I started hiking I felt as if I hadn't taken a deep breath in almost five years. I had been wearing my shoulders for earrings and they immediately dropped as I entered the forest.

My Polarity education taught me not only deeper wisdom of the elements and our connection to nature, but also a deeper understanding of our anatomy and physiology. One particular focus of anatomy and physiology is on our nervous systems, specifically the parasympathetic nervous system. This is the nervous system that is responsible for restoration and relaxation. This is where healing occurs.

Today many of us live in elevated stress states which take us out of parasympathetic states into sympathetic states. The sympathetic nervous system has no sympathy for you—its only focus is survival. It's what gets activated when we enter fight, flight, or freeze states. We are not meant to live in a sympathetic state full-time, yet many of us do. The author, Dr. Peter A. Levine, describes this as living in a suspended state of fear for prolonged periods of time, feeling as if the threat is always present.

I had been living in my sympathetic nervous system for a very long time, and transitioning into a rest-and-restore state took significant effort and practice. With the constant changing of homes, the packing, and the moving, I had become hardwired to being in fight, flight, or freeze and moving into relaxation wasn't easy and took consistent repetitive efforts. To this day I can feel when that familial flick of a nervous system switch is changed, and I have to go into repair mode to replenish and reset.

It wasn't just me. Once I recognized it in myself, I began to see this everywhere in my circles—people just couldn't relax. This indicated that we had all become slightly addicted to a state of being stressed. I know what you're thinking. Who would be addicted to stress? The problem is that we become so accustomed to our stress levels that it becomes comfortable. Our stress level seven essentially feels like a three. We don't notice the high level of stress because we're so used to it. The problem is that our nervous system certainly notices it, which is how we end up living with our sympathetic nervous system constantly activated. Then when our level of stress dares to be reduced, our body notices the change and immediately brings up any random thing so that we're back in our familiar state of stress. Feeling great this weekend? Wonderful. Now your body will bring up latent fears so that you drop back into a state of stress. And there goes your relaxing weekend.

During my hikes I felt free. I could cry if I needed to, laugh if something funny crossed my mind, rest from time on my devices, or send a voice note to myself for later journaling ideas. It was in nature where I felt I truly began to heal and feel like myself, or, the emergence of who I was becoming. Through each step I would remember to keep moving forward letting the path unfold before me. It wasn't a straight line. It was a winding series of elevation changes and ebbs and flows along the way. The trail symbolically reminded me of life and all its unknowns.

The path of growth is not linear but a series of ups, downs, twists, and turns. It takes time, as does the process of emerging through your metamorphosis. When I'd come across a group of butterflies taking off into the sunlight it would remind me that they didn't become a butterfly by accident. There was a process of becoming, with a whole lot of messy in the middle

Nature called me to silence and stillness. One afternoon I decided to pause on a bridge that crossed a creek. Something within me told me to draw my eyes level with the forest around me, an intuitive pull to be present to a moment. Right there in a small clearing was the most majestic whitetail deer I have ever seen. I had grown up around these animals, and I still feel a burst of excitement when I see them. I stood there for about fifteen minutes just watching the deer graze and be in its own environment nourishing itself on nature's bounty. No hunting was allowed in this park, and so this deer appeared to exist with little fear. It was just us two hanging out in a pocket of harmony together, the sun shining down on its grazing area. Like all things, peaceful moments come to an end. Someone came bustling down from a nearby trail scaring the deer off, ending our shared moment of stillness.

Sometimes it can be so loud inside us that we miss those whispers when the Seeker within nudges us and says: Look up, you don't want to miss this. In a world full of constant stimulation, it's no wonder we miss these moments. Peace and quiet are no longer something present throughout the day. Quiet evenings in front of a fire have been replaced by screens and scrolling. Walks to places in town are now filled with the noise of congested streets. The pockets of quiet that our ancestors had are gone. We have to create them for ourselves now.

When I got my new apartment, my priorities started to shift, and moments for peace and quiet went to the top of the list. I needed time to heal from heartbreak, and my focus was now on myself, no longer on maintaining or repairing a romantic relationship. Between yoga, my spiritual practice, or time in the woods, the space had been created for me to hear what the Seeker, Higher Self, Spiritual Guides, or God wanted to say. Turns out they were leading me toward travel and exploration.

In June of 2024 I hopped on a plane with a friend and headed to Lisbon for a week long holiday. We lost a day to traveling so there was no time to lose once we landed. I wanted to take a one day trip out to Sintra and visit the National Palace of Pena. It's this beautiful multi coloured palace up on the highest hilltop in Sintra and takes a good portion of travel time to get to on transit. I also researched that you can walk to the palace from the town of Sintra all the way up to the summit, which had me motivated to get a move on in the morning. An early hike meant less heat and a much more enjoyable experience for me. There were also two other places I wanted to see afterwards, so time was of the essence. This was obviously not a trail that I had ever taken before so I was truly walking into the unknown in a part of the world I've never been.

The trail started at the base of the town, and through each new stairwell and winding alley we eventually made it to the edge of the forest where cars were waiting to drive people to the top. "You don't need to walk there, let us drive you!" they pleaded. This was the "go, no go" point. If you don't take the car now, you're committed to the climb, so climb we did. My little 5'2 legs put the work in and we climbed and climbed. We took our time and at each new level of elevation stopped to take in the view. The shade provided by the trees thankfully created a cool environment to climb in; I couldn't imagine what it would've been like without the treetops offering shelter from the Portuguese sun. At one breathtaking stop, I thought about my family back home in Canada. If they tried to locate me on our family app I'd be a flashing little dot in the middle of the woods in Portugal. Something about that made me laugh and excited me. I was a little red faced and sweaty, but I was laughing. I was happy.

With each new stairwell came another turn in the road and a new sign to translate and keep us on track. I put my trust in Google Maps at a fork in the road, and I will never do that again. While I may have followed some path on Google it took us off road behind another group who also didn't know where they were going. After climbing over a large boulder that couldn't be a part of the path, we called it quits. We got off route somewhere and we needed to go back to the last sign and re-group. Covered in mud and some scrapes and bruises, we decided on a new direction, and back on the trail we got. A detour was taken and it's something her and I laugh about to this day. Life reminded me not to follow someone else's path. It may take you off course, but if it does you always have the choice to regroup and start again. The beautiful scenery, exercise, and ultimate experience was worth every step of the more than two hour climb to get from the base in Sintra to the palace at the summit.

Little did we know while at the base of the palace that there's still more climbing to do to get to the palace itself. And the car...well, we had no shame in our hiking game, but we were definitely taking it back down the mountain when it was time to go home. We did, and it only took us five minutes, dropping us exactly where we started hours before. Another thing we still laugh about.

T.S. Elliot, the poet and essayist, has a beautiful quote in his poem, *Little Gidding*. "We shall not cease from exploration and the end of all our exploring will be to arrive where we started and know the place for the first time." This verse rang through my entire being. When we started our hike that morning, I had no idea what I was about to physically encounter around each corner, what I would come up against emotionally, or what beauty I'd witness along the way. At the base of this staircase in Sintra, I began as one person—and I returned as another.

It was important for me to share this story because we can often get slightly off track on our spiritual journey. We may find ourselves distracted, misinterpret a sign, or even follow people heading in a direction to a completely different destination than us. The important part is to notice in your intuition when it doesn't feel right, then pause, discern, and regroup. There was no other option on our hike. We were in the thick of the forest, at least half way through and nearing the top. To keep on going became our only option, and that decision got us to our end destination.

The spiritual journey is similar to the experience I had in Sintra on the way to the palace. We began our climb without any idea of what was ahead. With continued effort we reached new levels of elevation and perspective. Somewhere along the way we got a little offtrack, but listened to our intuition and regrouped. We were tested and we persevered. We laughed about our detour and the scrapes and mud stains we picked up along the way. As we reached our destination we were ready to admit that it was okay to take a more scenic and relaxing way back after putting in all the work. It didn't always have to be a struggle. It's okay to do the work and enjoy the view. While the unknown can be scary, traveling always has a way of reminding us that the unknown can be pretty great too.

Nature continues to be one of my biggest teachers and also the place that grounds me the most during my spiritual journey. I can still smell the dampness of the forest in Sintra, see the freshness of the moss on the stone steps along the path, and feel the coldness of the large boulders that led our way to the palace. Those memories, the captured moments from my senses, are moments I can recall at the snap of a finger, using to further enrich my meditations and reflective moments. The peaks and valleys and not knowing what's coming around the next corner always serve as a metaphor and reminder in our lives. I would have missed many beautiful experiences on the way up had I not taken the path through the forest in Portugal.

People around the world are realizing the power that nature has in our lives. After a global pandemic and subsequent isolation, heading to the woods or your favourite nature spot is a great way to shake off some stagnant energy. Even sitting near some water can be enough to wash away some pressure in life and remind you of horizons yet to be seen.

The pandemic precautions prevented me from accessing the park for hiking so I spent time in the gardens that my landlord spent so much time in and surrounded myself with the flowers and beauty at my door-step. I would often be found laying next to the fountain looking up at the sky. "I see you out there, doing whatever it is you do," was something a neighbor said to me once. If he only knew. This is where I'd find myself in shavasana, and I'd let the ground below me hold up the weight of my fears and uncertainties. Sometimes I'd just listen to the water in the foun-tain, journal my thoughts, watch a movie on my laptop, or stare at the trees and try to single out the beauty in each leaf.

With isolation measures in place and travel restricted, I was, along with everyone else, spending a lot of time at home. I was finally reading through my untouched stack of books. I opened one written by the Bud-dhist nun, Pema Chödrön. *When Things Fall Apart: Heart Advice For Difficult Times.* How perfectly timed, I thought. It's a short and power-ful book about natural cycles and how our lives are filled with beginnings and endings. It reminds us of the cyclical patterns in life, and how we mirror nature's ebbs and flows. With each evening the sun goes down leading to darkness, only to rise again and begin anew, bringing the light with it. This can be used to remind us to embrace the darkness at the end of a cycle, accepting that light is on the way, beginning a new cycle in our lives.

One afternoon while lying in shavasana next to the fountain in the garden and periodically looking at the tree above me, I was reflecting on the uncertainty of getting back to "normal" when restrictions were lifted. I wondered if it was a normal I wanted to return to. With some more thought, I realized it wasn't. My time in Niagara was complete. Life was ready to show me something new, and I was excited for the road ahead.

Between 2012 when I moved to Niagara, to the summer of 2020 eight years later, I had discovered more about myself and spiritually than I could have ever imagined. Where I ended up looked wildly different from what was originally planned, and I left with no regrets. Over the course of the relationship, the breakup, changing jobs, moving homes, and the pandemic, I became an entirely different person.

Chapter Seventeen

RECIPE FOR BURNOUT

I was staring out the car window at a recently cleared field off the highway. I was thinking about how this new clearing would make for horrible road conditions come winter, which was something I dreaded every year. It was another exhausting day at work, and I was midway through my forty-five minute drive home. My wandering thoughts weren't the most optimistic.

I had grown accustomed to spending a lot of time in my car. At thirty six years old I was still driving the second car I'd owned. At the time it had over 350,000 km of history on it. When I moved to Niagara I would make the four hour drive home at least once a month. Because of that, I made a large playlist to keep me company. It was a lot of miles back and forth and the playlist helped pass the time.

I created it when I heard the acronym NET. I don't remember where I heard it, but the main focus was on removing the obstacle of "not enough time" when it came to doing reflection, reading, or being in my spiritual practice. Instead of saying that I didn't have enough time, I would find blocks in my day where I could fit in the audios or meditations that I wanted to listen to. The four hour drive back to my hometown or the forty-five minute drive home from work each day became my NET dedication slot, where I would fit in listening to my audiobooks or playlist that I had been putting off. Instead of listening to music the whole drive I would share the time with my practice, and sometimes just sit quietly the whole way and allow my thoughts to wander or settle.

I always do my most reflective thinking in the car. Many of my aha moments have been saved as voice notes on my phone so I can capture them in the moment and not leave to try to remember later. This particular afternoon I got into my car and felt utterly defeated. I was working in a corporate leadership job, and every difficult aspect of my leadership position seemed to be coming to a head. I was feeling the emotional weight of leading a group of hardworking people who were feeling unheard and exhausted. Made worse because all my efforts to support them were going unseen by my own leadership. As a female corporate leader I appreciated my position and the ability it gave me to hold space, empathize with the team, help each individual grow, cultivate a team atmosphere and company culture, and prove myself in a leadership role in an industry full of men. Unfortunately, I mostly felt the red tape of office politics cutting off the oxygen I needed to keep myself going in my own job, and felt I was holding the emotional weight of supporting the team on my own. It was beginning to weigh me down.

I came into this position during the pandemic. I made the decision to leave Niagara and move back home with my family. I had no regrets about that decision. It was the best thing for me, and I even got to help deliver the final beautiful baby girl that my sister had after missing the first three deliveries. I'll never forget the midwife asking me to help unwind the umbilical cord from around little Lydia's foot because the nurse wasn't able to make it in time. Travel limitations during the pandemic were complex. I made the decision to live with my family, save some money, and travel when borders reopened.

As months went on and restrictions continued to be in place I decided to get my own place. If I wasn't going to be travelling anytime soon, I may as well get comfortable and have quiet and privacy. This was a pivotal moment. Instead of continuously saving and building wealth, I chose comfort. Rentals had boomed during the pandemic and even with a full-time job the wealth I had accumulated seemed to disappear. A month after I moved into my apartment travel restrictions began to lift, and started to return to a pre-pandemic normal. Instead of breaking the new lease and traveling like I originally planned before the pandemic, I dug my heels in and stuck around. My pattern of being responsible even to the detriment of everything else was rearing its ugly head.

That decision to stay in my new home put me in a downward spiral. I was furious and disappointed in myself. I felt ashamed and began to beat myself up for becoming distracted from my dreams of travel and experiencing what the world had to share. But beneath that shame was something deeper; the realization that I had traded my travel savings for comfort. No, I couldn't predict the future, but I have a tendency to become impatient, often throwing me into misalignment. I had come a long way with my new job and caught on quickly, but felt disappointed in my leadership group so I stepped into a leadership role myself to hopefully be able to make some changes and help my team. My intentions were good and I even convinced myself it was what I wanted and was for the best, but there was a tightness within my stomach. I knew that by taking this new position, I was saying no to travel, one of my main priorities when I chose to move back home. Needless to say, I ignored that tightness in my stomach and did what I thought I was supposed to be doing to be responsible.

My inner voice was screaming at me and I blatantly ignored it. It was a clear "no" within me but I went my own way. I had now committed to renting my apartment and moving into this new role at work. You can imagine the tension that immediately came into my body as I intentionally chose misalignment in this phase of my life. I kept telling myself I needed to be responsible, see how this new position at work would play out, and fulfill my new rental agreement. But even my home wasn't a sacred place or decision. It was nothing like the "home temple" I had in Niagara. This was a "landlord special"—a quick coat of paint to cover the nicotine stained walls and quickly mudded patches on the walls without sanding. As I write this I can feel my shoulders hitting my ears, the tension in my muscles, and I shake my head wondering why I made those decisions. Looking back I question why I went so off track at this point of my life.

Actually, I can tell you why. It's simple. Can you guess what was missing from my practice during that time? Journaling. In the span of almost two years—maybe more—there's not a single journal entry. I meditated and listened to my audios, but not one word written down. The deeper reflections I would often work through in journaling were flying under the radar, and my ego, wanting security, was calling all the shots. When I get off track in life, it's usually because I've fallen out of my spiritual practice. And fall I did.

At every step I justified my actions, fell further into victimhood, and did what I could to convince myself that this was the right move, all while falling further into misalignment. This was a time when I sacrificed my passions and dreams and locked myself into someone else's. *"Be responsible... Take on more leadership at work... Live on your own... Be an adult... Your biological clock... Get something stable."*

While filling a leadership role may have been good for the company, it wasn't best for me. To offset the constant alarms and Teams notifications on my phone and computer, my only goal when I finally got home each night was to snuggle under my weighted blanket in a dark, quiet room. If I had it in me I'd muscle up the energy to jump into the shower to wash away the day, summoning some nearly empty reserve of energy for my dwindling personal life.

I was in this place of exhaustion and misalignment that evening driving home that I looked across to the newly cleared fields and had the less-than-pleasant thought about how miserable it would make the drive in winter. I was listening to Abraham Hicks and was hit with inspiration. All the energy I was spending during the day and each evening, plus all the recuperation time on weekends, was energy spent trying to force myself back into alignment. I knew it two years ago when I took the position and I certainly knew it now. This position was never a yes from me, and now two years later the effects of overriding my intuition were quite obvious. Regardless of my own state of being, I put effort into maintaining a level of professionalism, awareness, and emotional responsibility for my team and there was a price to pay for it all.

The audio that I was listening to was dedicated to getting yourself back into flow state and out of resistance. A flow state is generally described as a sense of ease, a trusting, or a feeling of surrender. In flow state things seem to come easier and appear to manifest into your life with little effort. Whereas resistance is described as frustration, obstacles, or force. Resistance feels like no matter how hard you try you don't progress, eventually becoming impatient with life. Alignment would be the equivalent to being in flow state and resistance would be its opposite, misalignment. This audio had me questioning how to move from being misaligned in many areas of my life—constantly forcing things and feeling frustrated at every turn—to coming back into alignment, where things felt easier and I could surrender to the flow.

I spent a lot of my day masking my exhaustion, which further exhausted me, of course. Trying to constantly return to alignment while simultaneously living out of alignment was a sure path to burnout. I was repeatedly saying yes to a life that felt like a no. I realized that I'd been here before. This was a pattern with previous jobs and relationships, but it wasn't until now that I put it together. I felt like my wheels were spinning and no walk in nature, nutritious meal, meditation, or nap could take away the fact that I was not living the life that I wanted. No leader can be a great leader if they're falling apart at the seams and don't want to be in that position anymore.

My strength in building connections, wanting to see people grow within themselves, and reminding them of their potential, will always be a keystone of who I am. But I knew I was ready to move on. Coming home each night to lose myself under my weighted blanket and sit in darkness to regulate my nervous system was not a reward I was proud of at the end of the day. I'd wrestle with my long-held desire to have kids one day and then wonder where on Earth I'd find the energy to parent a child when I felt this way. My weight skyrocketed, showing me that my body was rejecting my life and that it was time to return to myself and course correct. I had gone off-course and was lost in the metaphorical woods. I was giving everything I had to everyone else, yet when it came to what I gave myself, it was only the bare minimum, scraping the bottom of the barrel. Every yes to a no was a step that led me to burning out, and to an inevitable crossroads where I had to re-centre and choose myself again. Sounds like a repeated cycle for me, no?

No matter how off track you get, life will always bring you back to a point to course correct. Here it was, in the quiet of my car listening to Abraham Hicks. In fact, every morning presented a choice, and until that very day, it was a choice that I refused to acknowledge. My Seeker within knew what I had to do, but I hadn't been acting on the nudges. I had to own that I was choosing to stay in that job even though I could be doing something else to support my spirit and others in the world better. I was choosing to live a life with the mindset that I needed the job to cover expenses versus simplifying my cost of living. Each day I was creating stories around why I couldn't leave my position. I didn't want to let people down, but it was time to do what was right for me.

It only took a few more months before I knew the time had come. I was in the beginning stages of writing this book, was in a bit of a creative rut because of how burnt out I was feeling, and was sitting in our morning meeting at work. I heard the loudest voice within me say, "Today's the day." Clear as day. No hesitation. No questioning. Today was the day. I had done my best, but it wasn't the best for me. I effortlessly and confidently handed my notice to my boss and stepped down from my role. In truth, it had been written in my heart for months, but I printed, signed, and dated it that morning.

I'd be done in my position in two weeks. I was ready to reclaim my energy, and focus on writing. I had my sister on standby to remind me why I was making this decision in case fear took over and I tried to talk myself out of it. Turns out, her support services were not required. Proof that it was time and I knew it was the correct decision.

When you trust and believe in yourself, your decisions—emotional or not—become easier. After any life altering decision I've made, I've always become more resilient, stronger, and self assured. Alignment is the path to fulfillment and meaning, and misalignment becomes the path to exhaustion, resentment, and burnout. It doesn't mean that the path to alignment and authenticity is easy or devoid of tough decisions, but the end result is far richer and sustainable in energy and effort. It's listening to the yes or no within you and following it, not overriding it.

There's a tendency to stay in a situation far outside of its expiry date. To convince ourselves that our intuition was wrong this time. We hope things change. We hope it gets better. We hope that the situation itself will make a miraculous course correction. We hope, and we wait. While we wait, we put off living the life we want and are meant for. Sacrificing ourselves and our desires for anything out of alignment is a front row seat to burning ourselves out.

The stress of misalignment we place on ourselves is reflected in our cells, and the nervous system responds accordingly—leading to physical and mental health issues, including burnout or immune dysfunction. I've shared how impactful *When the Body Says No* by Dr. Gabor Matè was for me. His teachings on how our lifestyles and choices affect our health and overall wellness echoed constantly in the back of my mind. Each night, as I lay in the darkness under my weighted blanket, sympathetic nervous system running at full tilt, his words would rise up from within me as a reminder. No matter how hard you try to manipulate life into cooperating, if there are behaviours and ways of being that are not healthy for you, yet you try to force it, the body will remind you that you are one system, one soul, one body. The mind may rationalize or justify, but the body doesn't forget how it feels. It holds on to it all until it eventually manifests in ways you can no longer ignore.

For many of us, we have become accustomed to living separately from our bodies when it comes to decision making. We rely entirely on the mind, refusing to acknowledge how loudly our intuition and instincts can speak to us through our physical form. When we begin to listen to our intuition and act on truth, we simultaneously heal our relationships with our bodies. When we ignore our intuition, act incongruently from our truth, we disconnect energetically from our bodies, and live solely in the mind by overthinking, rationalizing, and justifying.

We become addicted to living comfortably in our uncomfortable lives, but in the back of our minds sits that gnawing sensation that something isn't right. No vacation, overtime hours at the office, or amount of distraction you employ will cause this to go away. It will sit there and wait for you to acknowledge it, and it will remind you of its presence at every opportunity.

We sit on decisions that we know are best for us because we are scared of the unknown. We sacrifice authenticity for an illusion of safety and security. Fear of change, the vulnerability of exposing our weaknesses, and even the admission and ownership of our faults can leave us hiding in the wings of our own lives. We avoid being seen with all our might, wearing our masks to blend in with the crowd. This level of survival, at our own expense, comes at a cost and will not disappear with the click of any ruby red heel. The only escape is through, and the only person you can take with you to an authentic, aligned life, is yourself.

Also, remember: your spiritual practice is specific to you. It's there to help you discover what lies beneath the surface, confront your patterns, and keep you emotionally and spiritually grounded throughout it all. If you find yourself metaphorically lost in the woods, and your practice has fallen by the wayside, there's one thing you can always do—start again and as many times as you need to. No self-judgement, no condemnation—just a gentle return to your practice. Picking your practice back up is far better than giving it up completely. It's perseverance over perfection.

As you can imagine and have seen through my story, and perhaps your own, the road to alignment and authenticity is not without its challenges. There comes a time when you have to stop and take account of where you're at and where you want to go. And there are times when there is nothing more to do other than pause. You may feel as if your wheels are spinning, and no matter how much you give, you feel empty in return. It's in those times that we need to put a hard stop on it all. We need to stop overworking, overgiving, overcompensating. We need to stop leaving ourselves on empty. Sometimes we need to cancel the plans, use the vacation time, and quiet the noise of life. We need to befriend our Seeker within and confront the messages that we've been desperately trying to avoid. When we stop forcing the messages away, we can finally listen to what they are trying to say and see what needs to change, so we can live authentically, purposefully, and in alignment. But to do that, we often have to stop and give ourselves a break.

Chapter Eighteen

REST STOP

O h My God! I lost my camera!" I realized that somewhere between the beach and the hotel, I must have absentmindedly left it behind. In hysterics, I traced my steps from the hotel to the beach looking for any lost-and-found with the hopes it was turned in. It was nowhere to be found. I'd borrowed that camera from a family member and now I'd lost it, along with all the photos from the days before. I knew I could replace the camera; the photos were lost forever.

I was fortunate to have had the opportunity to go to Hawaii with my high school basketball team. Our team, school, and community worked tirelessly to fundraise the money it cost for us to participate in a tournament there. I knew how much effort it took to get my team to the tournament, so each morning I woke up to the sunrise on Waikiki Beach in Honolulu, I was extremely grateful. I'd go to the local store, grab my shaved ice, and walk the streets in disbelief that I had made it to the island. Me, a wild child from a farm in Canada, was in Hawaii!

As part of the trip, we got to hike Diamond Head, the inactive volcano on the island. Looking up from down on the beach, this volcano was monstrous, covered in lush greenery, and looked as if its jagged edges were rising up from the ocean all the way to the sky. Its summit in the clouds enticing explorers. The hike allows you to climb all the way to the top, providing a picture perfect view of Honolulu spreading out below.

Unfortunately, the idea of "picture perfect" was all I focused on. I quickly snapped photos of nice views then immediately moved on without enjoying it because my competitive spirit had taken over. I wanted to be one of the first to the top. My focus became being in the lead, and my ego took over as I embarked on the unofficial race to the top. With each new corner or elevation I would snap a new photo and move onto the next. One click after the other, taking no time in between to take in the view myself. I trusted that I would look at the photos later when I had them developed. I rushed my way to the summit entirely missing the journey.

I made it to the top and celebrated with some girls from my team. I don't remember the view from the top—not one single memory of a stunning view comes to mind when I think about that day. And those photos that I was relying upon so heavily to enjoy the view later? Well, they were lost along with the camera the following day. I climbed this volcano in one of the world's most beautiful places, but I wasn't really there. I moved from moment to moment without looking up, down, or all around. There ended up being consequences.

I remember the views of the volcano from the beach. I had been looking up at it for days, counting down with excitement to the moment when we would begin our climb. The Seeker within me was at peak excitement levels and couldn't wait to begin the adventure. But when the day came, I dropped the ball. I missed the entire experience that I had been looking forward to for days. I let my competitive spirit take over by being solely focused on getting to the summit first. My ego created a story that being first to the top meant something about me, and that leading the pack was more important than enjoying the view.

I cringe when I think about that day and the choices I made. I am so disappointed that I missed out on something gorgeous because I was stuck in stories and expectations of my own creation. The lesson remains, though. We so often go from moment to moment without taking a breath, or stopping to smell the roses, or hibiscus, as you would in Hawaii, or enjoying the view, the journey, the experience. Our phones are in our faces from sunrise to sunset. We are focused on the next item on our to-do list, and then the next. We miss monumental moments with our friends and family because we aren't really paying attention, or are already thinking about something in the future. We don't listen in conversations because we are busy preloading a response.

From the moment we wake up we face countless transitions. We go from home to work, from work to home, and maybe something brief in between. We pull up in our cars, or exit the subways, and before we even walk in the door of the office we don't even stop to take an intentional breath to collect ourselves. We're just going, constantly moving. Thank God for our autonomic nervous systems that breathe for us when we forget to actively participate in taking a breath. From one conversation to the next it's a constant blur of interactions, emotions, and thoughts without a single pause in the day. We're an overstretched, overworked, and overtired society that doesn't take nearly enough time to pause.

Each transition presents an opportunity to pause, though. Taking a moment before your first coffee in the morning. Taking a deep breath when you exit your car before going into work. Stepping outside for fresh air during the workday and not taking out your phone. Shaking off the day before going to bed each night. It doesn't take much. Just pause for a moment to breathe. Drop your shoulders. Relax your jaw. Release any tension in your tongue, and breathe. Just breathe.

The daily grind and chase of success has moved rest down the list of priorities. I grew up hearing completely unhelpful phrases such as, "You can rest when you're dead," or "Rest is for the lazy." This created a negative belief about resting so I rarely did it. It wasn't until I caught myself repeating, "I can't stop; I have no time" and realized those weren't even my words. I had picked them up from someone else but had been allowing them to run my life for years. It was then I knew I needed to pause. When I noticed that phrase running circles in my mind I wondered what other "words of wisdom" I was living my life by. When I stopped and looked, I saw just how many things I had picked up from other people and were using their words, values, perspectives to create the roadmap of my life. The sneaky subconscious mind had struck again. Not only was this completely out of alignment for me, but trying to force myself to live within someone else's confines was exhausting and overwhelming.

Full schedules and overcommitting left almost no time for myself, and my lack of presence in my life became reflected in everything I did. From one family event to the next, I was always calculating my exit route rather than being present in the moment. I'd be busy factoring in how long it would take me to get there all while missing the human connections around me, or opportunity to connect with another person at my table. I'd also be distracted from being present for the host, the person who was celebrating and who had invited me to be there. I'd physically be there, but I wasn't present, not really. The thoughts racing through my mind were subtly pulling my consciousness out of the room, and leaving my body filling the chair at the table.

I found my way to Ekhart Tolle's teachings around 2015. I had heard of this man before, but at the time I didn't feel called to pursue his teachings. Sometimes it's just not the right time. I had come back around to his work when *The Power of Now* came out. I was drawn into the idea of being more present in my life, slowing things down, and being more intentional with my choices and thoughts. I was tired of barely being an active participant in my life, showing up in portions rather than wholly, giving my friends and family my bare minimum. The thin size of *The Power of Now* was also attractive at the time. Short and sweet. I thought, perfect, and straight to the point. Waste no time, right?

I was motivated to read the book when I noticed I had been missing the mark in a lot of places in my life. I'd bring my work life into my home, and I'd bring my home life into my workplace. Was I ever fully present in the place that I was, whether it be work, home, or out in public?

I started to give myself more time in the mornings to set a tone for the day. If I left the house in a rush it felt as if I had fallen over a hurdle, unable to recover mentally until lunch time. I'd use every opportunity at work to get still, pause, and rest. At lunch you probably would have found me with my legs up on the wall, or taking deep breaths doing everything I could to decompress. I used my time in the day deliberately and with intention to focus on being present. Being more present became my only goal, and in becoming more present I began to see life more clearly.

With over-stretching and over-scheduling came the over-thinking. My mind was constantly running on overdrive, yet my body was running on fumes. I was getting sick multiple times a year. I began to understand that just because I can do something doesn't mean I should. Just because I could fit everything in and try to be everything all at once doesn't mean that it was healthy. I was sick because I wasn't taking care of myself. Slowly but steadily, every commitment and exhausted decision I made, would show physically. I would get sick. Have to take antibiotics or steroids, usually followed by another round of antibiotics. I'd take sick days from work, but I wasn't resting, merely recovering. I would return to work just as exhausted and knew I would need to wait until I had a vacation planned to finally and fully rest. The vicious cycle would continuously play itself out. Exhausted. Sick. Recovering. Unrested. Exhausted. Sick... I couldn't outrun it, no matter how hard I tried, and it took me a while to finally understand what was happening.

As I continued to understand the importance of presence in our lives, I saw that it needed to be a holistic approach. From the moment we wake up we are granted a choice to be present for the day ahead. The way we show up for others and the way we process information through our senses changes by the level of our presence. By not being present we leave ourselves open to being reactive to life's surprises, which results in us acting from the limiting beliefs and fears that exist within our subconscious minds. When in reactivity, we douse our nervous systems with stress chemicals, wreaking havoc that can take years to heal from.

By being present in our lives, we give ourselves the permission to choose our response. It keeps us from playing a blame game, thinking that someone else made you do something or that something someone else said triggered a knee-jerk response from you. With presence is ownership of self, dominion over your behaviour, and ultimate sovereignty of your mind, body, and spirit. It puts the "response" in "responsibility." To be present is to be mindful of the energy you choose to embody and the thoughts you let yourself believe and attach to. It doesn't mean that we ignore what's presented to us, or the fact that someone has hurt us or that we are in disagreement. What presence says is: I see what's happening and I'm choosing how I want to show up here.

When we are present with ourselves, we can be present for others.

I've found that when I am fully present people naturally open up to me. It's as if they can tell they're sharing a moment with me, one that is fleeting that we're both here for. And in that space that we're both present for, inhibitions dissipate, masks get taken off, and authenticity shines through. There is a comfort in sharing presence with someone, and it is intuitively felt. But it must start with you. When you are present, the people you will be with will probably be more present too.

With presence, there's no judgement or pressure. In the power of presence, connection is possible. Society has grown accustomed to disconnecting from each other in fear that eye contact with the wrong person may put their safety at risk. What if you were the person on the train who was aware of their surroundings, ready to help someone in need, able to step in to protect someone whose safety is at risk, or give up your seat for the elderly man who boarded in the back. With our headphones on and our eyes glued to our phones we miss out on opportunities to connect with one another. We miss the moments of connection of what could be someone's final day on Earth.

There's a story I once heard about a young man who, in his darkest moment, sat alone at a Waffle House on Christmas night. He'd made peace with ending his life—but one stranger's story across the table cracked something open in him. It reminded him that love is a two-way street. That even in the depths of despair, connection—even with a stranger at Waffle House—can save us. Because of that connection, and the revelation that presented itself in that sacred moment, he chose life.

That story stays with me. It's a reminder that the Seeker within us is always listening and paying attention—but also always waiting for us to do the same. We miss the moments that happen in connections with other people when we aren't paying attention. We miss the hints from the story being shared by a stranger that could be the missing puzzle piece to help end the suffering within our own lives. What if the Seeker only needs your full attention for a few minutes a day to remind you of something, or provide you with wisdom to benefit your life? Those few moments of connection with the Seeker within can be the exact moments you need to pause all the "overing"—overcommitting, overthinking, overanalyzing.

I had an overwhelming tendency of working through my breaks and my lunch in my corporate job. This inevitably made me cranky, energetically drained, and mentally absent by the end of the day. Slowly, and with daily discipline I started taking my breaks to recoup some of the energy I would lose in the day. I'd either sit outside with my feet in the grass, relax in a reclining chair, or head out to my car for solitude. Sometimes I would disappear into a quiet space in the office and just rest. I used every minute of my break to rest, refocus, and come back refreshed.

I felt that this small change made me a better person and leader. Carving out this time taught me that rest is not a luxury nor for the lazy, but a necessity in sustaining my wellbeing at work and at home. If I prioritized my wellness at work I genuinely had a more enjoyable and energized evening at home. It helped me show up alert for my team, and feel fully available to an employee looking to chat or connect in the privacy of my office. I wouldn't be stretching myself thin, or struggling to listen to them, or giving off distracted energy. I got to be an active part of the conversation, connect with my team, and ultimately be more productive than on the days I let the chaos sweep me off my feet.

One day, I was lying in my lounge chair during my break and staring out the window. My truths would often bubble to the surface when I would sit like this and just look outside. Staring gently out the window is often how I assume a meditative state. Thoughts of travel had occupied my mind, and I realized that the dream I had to experience new parts of the world and culture had become a distant memory. I hardly recognized who I had become, and while I felt successful in my job there was this aching and yearning to return to my personal goals, images of past vision boards and destinations floating to the front of my mind. I was feeling called to return to who I once saw myself becoming and all the possibilities that brought with it. I was feeling the familiar signs of burnout, work was showing no signs of slowing down, and to top it off, it was the dead of winter. I couldn't sit outside, and seasonal depression courtesy of a Canadian winter was kicking my ass. I needed the pause, and I took the time to just breathe. My break timer sounded off, breaking my sweet reverie, and I headed back to work.

That afternoon I had an email come through on my phone. The break I had taken must have dropped me into alignment. The International Polarity Education Alliance was hosting their first conference since the pandemic, and it was being held in Glastonbury UK. "Um, what's this? Yup, I'm doing that!" It had been years since I had a vacation, and I was feeling the result of not using that time and getting away. Not only was it an opportunity to go somewhere new, live my dream of travel, but it was also a chance to connect with Polarity Therapy practitioners from around the world. I'd be in a group of people who understood how profound Polarity Therapy was. I made a decision to take a break from it all and dust off my passport. UK, here I come!

Ultimately, it felt like the perfect opportunity for me to reconnect with myself, restore my energy, and realign with who I wanted to be. I had thrown my hands up, and admitted that I needed a break. I had an undeniable feeling that Glastonbury was exactly where I needed to be. Within days I had an entire trip planned to England. When you align with something, it feels as if there's not one single obstacle that could stand in your way. What I didn't know was how life changing Glastonbury would end up being, and what healing and transformational experiences were about to come my way. But for now, I knew this: the pause had led me back to possibility.

Chapter Nineteen

GLASTONBURY

If I wasn't driving I would have been hanging out the window like a child. To say I was excited was an understatement. That fact that I hadn't gotten lost on the way had me feeling like a million bucks. My confidence was soaring. You could see it from a distance. Rising out of the mist was the unmistakable silhouette of the Glastonbury Tor, crowned by St. Michael's Church. I had seen it in photos, obsessed over it for years, sat in awe for months knowing I was going to be there, but being able to see it from afar was breathtaking. To know that was my destination, I was over the moon.

Glastonbury is known more in the modern world for its large festival that takes place every year. Thousands make their way out to the area to enjoy music and global artists, lights and fireworks, over the course of five days. More traditionally it's known as being Avalon. The history is steeped in mythology and folklore. The Isle of Avalon, or the Islands of Avalon, has been said to be home to the Holy Grail and King Arthur and his mystical sword, Excalibur. There's an eccentric and historical energetic hum that is noticeable upon arrival. It is unmistakable in every winding road and alleyway. Glastonbury has a presence all its own.

I had flown into Heathrow in London, rented a car, and made my way out of the city toward Glastonbury. The contrast between the two locations was vast. The hustle and vibrancy of London was nothing at all like the quiet and serenity of Glastonbury.

I was reeling off of my whirlwind days of travel. Driving on the opposite side of the road had me feeling like I was going backwards through traffic circles, winding my way along the narrowest roads I've ever seen, and having my stomach in my throat behind the wheel, which is also on the opposite side, that by the time I finally arrived in Glastonbury I wanted to stop the car, unload my bags, and not move for a week. But I was here for a reason.

My day of arrival marked the first evening for the International Polarity Education Alliance's conference. That night I would head up to the historic Abbey House where it was hosted, check-in, and meet the other attendees. Nervously, I walked through the gate and into a large group of other practitioners. I knew no one. Not one person in that room of practitioners was someone that I had met before, but I knew and held within me that every single person there had something in common. Polarity Therapy brought us all together.

Nervously, I made a cup of tea. That's what they did in England right? "Act normal," I told myself while trying not to laugh thinking about Ted Lasso and his feelings about tea. I checked in and said hello to others in the room. That was a good place to start right? Every moment was brand new, it was as if I was figuring out how to interact for the first time in my life. I was surrounded by different languages, and high-tailed away from people that seemed to be speaking in similar tongues. "Were they speaking Polish? I think those two are Swiss, no wait that was German, no wait that was French. What? What am I doing here?" This was the conversation happening in my mind as I tried to find "my place" in the group. The blend of different European countries and languages felt intimidating. Out of a back room came the organizer and fellow practitioner, Phil Young. His deep belly laugh followed by, "Hello my friend!" was unmistakable and immediately put me at ease.

I continued to introduce myself to others, more people filed in, and we settled into an adjoining room for opening remarks along with a presentation from Phil and another brilliant practitioner, Morag Campbell. Her name had been shared amongst my Ontario group of practitioners and was held in high regard by my own teacher Sher Smith back home.

Their collective presentation immediately reminded me that I was exactly where I needed to be. They spoke about the energy of the planet and why they chose Glastonbury. The Tor represented the masculine and the nearby Chalice Wells represented the feminine. They were amongst the top reasons, but not the sole reason why they chose this eccentric place. The belief that the Earth has significant energetic hot spots or chakras around the world is not lost in Glastonbury. Like the Pyramids in Egypt, Mount Shasta in California, or Lake Titicaca in Peru, Glastonbury emits an energetic frequency that many pilgrims and people today still feel drawn to. There is a belief that energetic ley lines within the Earth itself have created a hub, an energetic center or chakra, right there in Glastonbury. Specifically, pilgrims connect to Glastonbury by way of the energy of the Heart. People searching for healing or a sense of connection to something greater often feel inspired to visit here—like the land itself invites you to let go of the old and make space for something new. And making space for something new... that sounded pretty good to me.

They continued speaking about the historical draw to Glastonbury and the connection humans naturally have to nature and the heavens. The conversation in the room centered around the idea that for the majority of humans, we have become disconnected from our planet. The ego's main drive for material things and power has cut our energetic connection off at the heart. We've forgotten that we originally came from the Earth and that we are tied to it energetically. By being in tune to nature we keep energy in balance. This is true for its opposite. When we fall out of tune with nature, balance is lost—in the natural world and within ourselves. The question of how we reset this energy within us—and who was going to help us do it—was posed to the room. We looked around at each other, and the room filled with quiet laughter, because we knew that we had volunteered for the job.

This is the type of conversation that excites me. Mainly, because these are not the discussions I would have around my dinner table growing up, nor was it the type of conversation I would overhear at any local cafe. It's a complete perspective shift and shift in consciousness on the way we can view life and how we show up in it. We ended the night with a final word from Dr. Stone, the founder of Polarity Therapy: "We know there's a relationship of the outside world or universe with ourselves. The universe is the reservoir or source of our supply, that is definite. Our life on this planet depends for its existence on our ability to draw from it each moment exactly what we need." This echoed my internal call. I would often return to nature for solace and refuge during uncertain times—and it always provided exactly what I needed.

The days ahead would be conversations around moving energy through the body, releasing trauma, sacred geometry and its history through time. Amongst all of the theory-based learning was what many look forward to the most, bodywork. Imagine a room filled with twenty or so massage tables spread out spanning from wall to wall. In my Polarity classes and clinical weekends we would have multiple session tables set up, but I had never seen this many tables in a room, and in the type of location that we were in. The historic building of Abbey House, while being largely retained in its Tudor Gothic features, created a backdrop of serenity and calmness that I had never experienced during a session.

Behind Abbey House were the ruins of Glastonbury Abbey itself, one of the main sites in the small town. Abbey House had been built to overlook the abbey ruins, making the view part of its historical charm. Behind the massage tables and in view through the large windows were the ruins of the abbey dating back to 1539. At the back of Abbey House there were the most magnificent gardens. Calla lilies the size of my palm and roses the size of my fist grew in plenty. Local cats meandered around and pheasants flew from tree to tree. If you stood still, were really present, and looked down towards the ruins of the abbey, you could feel history and the energy of Glastonbury pulsating through the air right through you and all around. It felt as if I existed between two worlds, history on one end, and the mystery of what was to come on another.

The second day a schoolmate of mine, while originally hailing from England, joined me from Ontario. We had spent countless hours together completing our studies, working diligently every week to cross off our additional compulsory and supplementary work, as well as many weekends together for classes. We met while both living in Niagara, but having left during the pandemic, I hadn't seen her in years. We reminisced at a local pub about how far we had both come. We had taken our first year at separate times, and our paths came together for the second year. She reminded me about where I was when I had first reached out to her. I had been living with my ex, and as you now know I was also on the precipice of a major life change. From the moment I said hello, Silvana Vega never left my side. Here we were almost ten years later in Glastonbury at a local pub attending an international conference. It was a full circle moment for us. We toasted to our resiliency, to listening to a calling, and to our friendship.

Conference days were jam packed. The following two days were twelve hours full of theory, body work, sacred geometry, trauma regulation, and movement. One presenter after the next shared their wisdom and experience with us. We had scheduled time to nurture our bodies, see the sites, and integrate the new knowledge we were taking in. The Abbey House blessed us with nourishing meals—some of the most beautifully presented foods that I had ever seen. Again, vibrancy on a plate. I couldn't help but chuckle at how the practitioners from the west were adding more salt to their food. I thought it was just me, and this was the first time I noticed a difference between European and Western food. Between the nourishment we were provided during breaks, and the nourishment of knowledge, I felt full of everything that this life had to offer.

The third day of the conference was a day that forever changed me. With the full itineraries required for the conference, I made it a point that I would take some time and climb the Glastonbury Tor. I had been in keynotes and sessions each day for twelve hours a day, and a Tor climb would not be scratched out from my personal to do list. Once the conference was done I had plans to move on to a new location so the schedule for sightseeing here in Glastonbury was tight. The land below the Tor would have been flooded at one time, and as the locals shared the lore of the Mists of Avalon more and more, there was no way I wasn't going, and early in the morning was the best time to go. Between walking there, climbing to the top, and getting back in time for the conference, there was no time to spare.

I began my journey and walked through the quiet streets of Glastonbury. Many in town were still quietly asleep, and only a few other dedicated walkers and local sheep met me along the way. The quietude was a stark contrast to the streets at high noon, full of day-trippers and shoppers. I walked through town and made it to the base of the Tor. With it being a well-known historical site I thought this would be a well defined parking lot, but in reality it was a tree covered trail entrance with a rock that simply stated "Tor." Assuming I was going the right way, I made my way up. One turn became another staircase, which led to a gradual incline. That incline led to another staircase and so on. You get it.

About halfway up, red cheeked and huffing and puffing I noticed three women. They were taking their time, and I could faintly make out music. One woman in the group was softly playing what resembled a ukulele while singing what sounded like a Celtic ethereal song. It was as if she was serenading my pilgrimage to the top, and I was secretly grateful for having climbed the moment that I did. It was a beautiful way to experience this moment. It was unexpected and had me cherishing each step just a little bit more. As I closed the distance between them I looked out over the view, and the town of Glastonbury was barely visible through the mist. St. Michael's Church at the top of the Tor was getting closer and closer.

As I arrived at the top I was taken aback by the landscape around me. The sun was rising just as I ascended, and I can remember every detail of the farm fields below and the sounds of the local roosters and sheep waking their farmers. I'd learnt the hard way in life to be present for these moments, and I wanted every detail to be solidified in my memory for the rest of my life. I wasn't relying on a camera to capture these moments for me. I was fully present—taking in each smell, the serene scene below, and sounds of wildlife contentedly living out their days on the farm. For about thirty minutes or so I took in the view, and ventured my way back down the other side of the Tor. I made my way through local roads, and even local sheep fields. Small gates allowed access to pedestrians as long as you closed it behind you. Each moment I took care to not step in a gift a local sheep left behind. It was a beautiful way to start the day, anchored me to the present, and I was glad to have checked something off my tourist to-do list.

That morning at the conference we spoke about trauma. We witnessed one of our members assisting another in releasing a traumatic experience that they still felt within the body. It amazes me what two people can accomplish in a session while working in tandem, when one is open to supporting and the other open to receiving. It was a beautiful site to witness, and the emotional release from the receiving member was a vulnerable and brave moment of transformation that we got to be a part of.

We had been given an extension for our lunch hour, and my friend Silvana and I decided to take an adventure up the road where the red Chalice Well was located. People pilgrimage from all over the world to the Chalice Well for the fresh spring water that you can collect. It is believed to have healing powers. Mythical accounts suggest that Mary Magdalene hid the Holy Grail, or chalice, within the Chalice Well itself. It is said that the Holy grail was used to collect the blood of Christ at the Crucifixion, and that the reddish hue within the water of the Chalice Well symbolises the rust of the nails on the cross and the blood of Christ.

As we headed out from Abbey House the rain gently started coming down. Not letting it stop us we carried on until we made it to the gates of the Chalice Well. I purchased a few extra glass bottles. This way I could bring home some water from the spring, which the attendant had shared was full of minerals, and to drink it slowly. My intention was to bring it home, and drink it before my meditation practice. The garden surrounding the well was still lush and bright with different flowers and plants. Although it was raining, the mature trees surrounding the well provided dry space to sit and reflect from. Small trinkets were hidden within the trees and on ledges throughout the garden pathways. People would bring offerings of thanks to the well, or totems to reflect their faith, and to show their dedication to Christ as well as Mary Magdalene. Women from all over the world travel to the Chalice Well to offer up their acknowledgement of women's power and role in spirituality and in history.

We made our way through the gardens and came across the Lion's Head Spring. This was where we filled up our bottles and grabbed handfuls of water to quench our thirst. I'll admit that after I read and heard some of the local lore surrounding the well I couldn't help but feel that this moment was a powerful one, and that being here and drinking directly from this spring ignited a strength within me that I didn't know I had.

Two years earlier, I had read *Mary Magdalene Revealed* by Meggan Watterson, and at that moment, I felt extremely close to Mary and Jesus. She was a woman who had been dragged through the mud for years within the Christian tradition, but she was so much more than history made her out to be. As a spiritual woman myself, I felt a deep connection with her and her path. And as a woman working in a male-dominated industry, I had come to appreciate her leadership. The connection between Jesus and Mary brought a balance of masculine and feminine energies into my faith. I splashed cool water on my face and wet my hair. It felt like a rebirth—a refreshing of my faith, a baptism of sorts. The cool water from the well seemed to awaken something deep within my spirit. I understood that I shared this spot with many pilgrims, and I was no different. If Mary really had been here then it would be something that connected us through time. I even took a moment to notice the essence of polarity on the lid of the well. The two intersecting circles create a neutral center, with the masculine and feminine poles resting at the top and bottom of the lid. Polarity, as life reminded me, exists everywhere, and balancing these energies is essential for harmony in life. With the afternoon moving quickly we said goodbye to the well hoping to make it back one last time before we left.

I was feeling agitated that afternoon at the conference. My lower back was in pain. I could not get comfortable no matter what I did. Left and right I would volunteer as tribute and be the guinea pig for any bodywork that came up, yet was unable to get called to a table. The rain was coming down harder, and the day just felt dreary. I couldn't tell if this was pain from jet lag and driving across England, sleeping on beds that weren't my own, sitting in chairs all day, or emotionally feeling the exhaustion from flooding my brain with too much information. Likely all of the above. Whatever it was, I was grumpy, I was judgmental of other people in the room and their questions, and I was upset with myself. My ego was having a field day. What was going on? This was not like me—I'd started the morning with a beautiful calm before all of this. We made it to afternoon break, and I thought maybe I was just hungry and the feelings would pass. Not a chance. If anything the volume in the break room was setting me off more, and I knew I just needed some peace and quiet.

I made my way to the room where all the session tables were set up, and I laid myself down facing up to the ceiling. I closed my eyes, took a breath, and took a break. Slowly I turned to my right side, and along with it allowed my left leg to slowly drape across my body and hang gently off the side of the table. With that one slow gentle movement, and the assistance of gravity, I felt the largest adjustment that my lower back has ever received. With each lumbar vertebrae adjustment I felt the tension in my back subside, and as I returned to neutral on my back I was flooded with relief. At that moment, nothing could stop my tears as they slid down my face. I gave myself exactly what I needed, and the relief was incredible. I listened to the call to find a table and listened to my body and followed its desire for a gentle movement. I had everything I needed, and the relief after days of built up tension slowly faded from my body.

As I laid on the table allowing myself to enjoy the moment, two other women walked into the room. "Do you mind if we pop in and do some work?" Of course I didn't mind; the more healing in the room the better. That's what we were there to learn and do. I continued to lay in my space and started to feel waves of emotion running through me. The release in my back opened the floodgates of my eyes and I just let it go. I had been reflecting over my day and how special it was. From climbing the Tor and drinking directly from the Lion Head Spring of the red Chalice Well, to returning to the conference with these people, I couldn't help but feel overcome with gratitude for the experiences I'd had and the life I was living. Ten years ago, if you had told me this would be my life—when I was spiritually crumbling in my relationship, emotionally defeated in the tub, and feeling like a stranger in my own home—I would have wanted to believe you, but don't think I could have.

The two women finished up, and as the one member went to take her leave she noticed my state. She gently walked up to me, leaning down to my side and asked "Is this physical pain you're feeling?" I shook my head no and she jumped into action. Because we were both present with each other at this exact moment, a moment of deep emotional release was about to be unleashed. She was ready to support, and I was ready to receive. She sat behind me, laid her right hand on my forehead, and her left hand underneath the back of my head, and I let the full weight of my head fall into her palm. She held me as I released all the tension from my neck and shoulders. I sobbed—deep, uncontrollable sobs. The kind that takes two inhales just to match one exhale. With each powerful exhale, it felt as if my chest lifted off the table.

At first I tried to hold it, but then quickly dismissed it. I thought to myself, "if I can't do this here, then where can I?" I knew I needed this release. I let go fully, and completely disregarded any worry if others in another room could hear my sobs. It was as if my cries had been trapped inside me for a lifetime begging to get out. The energy center of my own heart was letting go of years of unexpressed emotion.

Another member entered the room from the dining area, and spoke with the practitioner supporting me. In mere moments she jumped in and lightly held each one of my ankles. As soon as she joined I let go even more. I didn't even know who it was then—it didn't matter. If I thought I was grateful before, I was surely grateful now. My heart burst wide open, my emotions flowing out like the water in the well itself. Flashes of Lion's Head Spring came rushing through my mind. I couldn't hold anything in, still trying to catch my breath between sobs. I was across the world in a building full of people who I didn't know but knew how to be there for another person, and right now, they were there for me. At a time when our world feels so disconnected, I was surrounded by like-minded individuals who purposefully connected with those around them—without fear, hesitation, or judgement. In that room, I felt undeniably safe and unashamed.

I was further instructed to lay on my left side, and as I turned over she gently placed her right hand over my sacrum on my lower back. I was facing the window and through my tears and the pouring rain on the windows I could faintly make out the silhouette of the abbey ruins. The raindrops reminded me they were only there because the clouds let them go, and it was time for me to release all that I had numbed and repressed for years. "As above, so below," I thought—a phrase I used often in my Polarity classes and a lens that I viewed the world. Life was always reminding me of our connection with it. The macro above—life itself—surrounded me, offering a new lesson to the micro below: me. And in this moment, I had never felt so connected or present in my own life. Still, I sobbed. Images of wandering London, climbing the Tor, and drinking from the Chalice Well flooded my mind. Having this emotional moment in front of the ruins of the Abbey, surrounded by these incredible practitioners from around the world, overwhelmed me.

For so much of my life, I felt like an anomaly—never quite fitting in, always a little different, sensitive, or intense—as if it were a bad thing. At that moment, I felt free. I realized that being or feeling like an anomaly was actually a pretty great thing. It suddenly became clear to me that an anomaly means something rare, something going against the grain, or something hard to replicate. Here, I finally felt proud of who I am and every step I took to get here. Some people can live this life and say that they have been blessed, and I am one of them. As I lay on my side, looking out through the windows at the abbey ruins, sobbing my heart out, I knew that I had been truly blessed. Nature—again—delivered to me in that moment what it always does, always has, and always will: clarity. That moment in Abbey House, and the events leading up to it, were a blessing. Whatever hardened shell had surrounded my heart dissolved into stardust, chipped away by love, self-acceptance, human connection, nature, and life's love for me—and my love for it.

The final presentation was about to take place and waves of emotion kept coming. I signaled to the ladies that I was good, thanked them greatly and gave them an embrace. Before she left, the original member said to me "You are cared for, I just felt the need to tell you that," and she left the room. I've learnt to honour my emotions as they come up, and for the next forty minutes they did. I continued to release tears of sadness, repressed grief, and gratitude. I took a moment to acknowledge her parting words and years of my life flashed before my eyes where I hadn't felt cared for or forgotten. I eventually gathered myself, grabbed my journal from my bag, exited through the back door, and found a dry place to sit in the cozy gardens. I wrote about my experience and let it wash over past pain and heartache with forgiveness and understanding, making room for something new. The sun was setting as I watched the sunlight fade on the abbey ruins and disappear into the night. Eventually, I returned to the room, catching what remained of the final presentation.

As I walked back to the flat that night, through the darkened streets of Glastonbury, I reflected on all the moments that had brought me here. At one point, I almost didn't follow my call into Polarity Therapy. I even found myself ready to give up on my dreams of travel—at one point, I nearly gave up on myself entirely. Every hurt from my past, every inspirational moment, and every curious question led me to exactly where I needed to be. I believed that I had experienced a true blessing from life—and that life wants us all to feel blessed. To do that, *we need to walk in step with it.* I was reminded again that relationships—whether with life or with the Seeker within—are a two way street, and many of us are walking in the opposite direction, away from the blessings that await us.

Before all of that, was a call to pick up a seemingly random book from a bookshelf at my Nanny's retirement home. *Soul's Perfection* taught me how to look within, and how to listen to that inner voice when it spoke up. It taught me to trust and to believe that I was loved and being guided. The Seeker within me led me to Glastonbury, but it was the choices I made and ideas I put into action that actually got me there. The Seeker and I had worked together to get here. While inspiration can come and go, your responsibility of doing the things that inspire you is what will ultimately get you where you want to be. Inspiration without action are dreams that fade or continue to poke you from within for a lifetime. I'd leave Glastonbury a changed woman being more open, energetically lighter, and more inspired for the life and challenges that were yet to come. The Heart Chakra of the planet delivered, and sent me off to live my life.

Chapter Twenty

HEADS UP

A s I sit to write this final chapter, I glance over the stacks of books I've collected through the years. When I take my time and scan over them I can recall where I was spiritually when I purchased each one of them. My bookshelves have become symbolic of the timeline of my spiritual growth. Some purchases were driven by my ego's desire to appear more spiritual, having no idea what the author was saying until many years later when I had a better understanding. *"Bhagavad Gita-whatta?"* I'd joke to myself, realizing how out of my depth I was. Some I've read and felt as if I could toss it right in the bin, but years later when I would pick it up again it became a staple in my personal growth. I've remained open to the teachings of many who've walked before me, and in that openness, I've found a little bit of truth in each one—truth that spoke to me. Nuggets of wisdom from Jesus, the Buddha, and the Taoist philosopher Lao Tzu have helped shape the way I view life just as much as those I've mentioned earlier in the chapters. There are countless books about being a high performer and optimizing every moment of my life, and others that remind me that striving for high achievement meant nothing to me if I felt disconnected from my soul and spirit.

Through each book, I recognize different phases in my life, with dedication to spirituality as the core factor of everything I've done. I see manuals in my office, or workbooks from weekend workshops from times in my life when I felt my inner light dim. With each new book and mentorship I'd learn something new and find what did and didn't work for me in my spiritual life. The majority of the works within my collection were purchased when I was in the middle of an experience, or at the beginning of becoming aware of the unexpected lesson that I was meant to learn.

When I made my final move back home from Niagara there was an afternoon that I spent packing up all my books. With each book I'd pick up I'd remember when I bought it. I noticed a theme that I hadn't purchased many of them just out of curiosity. I had purchased it because I was in the middle of trying to understand what I was experiencing during a new transition or lesson in my life. "A heads up would have been nice!" I said out loud. It was loud enough and sassy enough I hoped God, guides, and all the Universe heard me. While looking at all my books, something didn't sit right. Did we really have to learn as if our journey was one surprise lesson after the other? Did it really have to take an age to uncover personal truths or that helping prep someone for the journey ahead was a secret? The heads up of what could happen, was missing from my bookshelf and subsequently, my experience. Everything felt so unexpected, difficult, and reactive. I wish I had at least known a few things to look out for. I didn't notice any books upon my shelves about what I might possibly encounter along the way in my spiritual journey. That's what was missing from the books I'd read. I wanted something that could have helped me anticipate some of the stages ahead on my spiritual journey instead of learning on the fly.

I reflected back on the people that I had met in recent years. I thought about how so much had been shared at events, or online spiritual groups that sounded similar. "Ya, I've been through that," or "You haven't seen anything yet," referring to deep transformations, and the moments of life that are completely overhauled. I'd see someone post online what their current experience was and someone would respond "Oh ya, that's the Dark Night of the Soul. Have fun with that." What? We were just leaving people in this limbo of uncertainty after dropping this unknown term on them. It's an equivalent experience of having a symptom and going to Google for your diagnoses, and being surprised that it created more anxiety than a clear path or some inner peace.

It motivated me to publish a book that provided the reader the heads up that I wish I had when I started out. I was young when it began, online communities hadn't been created yet, at least none that I was old enough to join, and I had to learn so much on my own. I learnt about topics as they came up in my life, but nothing had really been laid out to help in preparation. Something that let me know that I may encounter XYZ, or to be able to feel that *this* is what they meant by Dark Night of the Soul. A heads up would have been helpful. While self discovery and the spiritual life has an essence of surprise and unexpected turns, I didn't believe that it needed to feel as if you were flying blind all the time.

The intention of this book was to feel like a mentorship tool for you as you begin your own journey. I wanted to give you the awareness and information to be proactive in a way that I never could be. My goal was to provide you with a reminder to come back to the fundamentals when you start to over-complicate your spiritual journey or try to control it. I wanted to give you a basic idea of what to expect at certain points along the way. I wanted you to have what I never did.

Countless nights I lost sleep over the uncertainty of what was to come. Lying awake staring blankly at the ceiling thinking I couldn't take much more. When people would say, "Oh, just wait for what's coming," it was never encouraging or helpful, and if anything it made my ruminations worse. Can the spiritual journey include a possible road map of events, stages, or tips so we can get behind our growth with excitement, or at the very least, a little peace of mind over the unknown? Could we surrender with a little more trust in the process if we had a little heads up? Those are the questions I hope to have answered through this book.

It can feel uneasy when you start to become more aware of yourself and surroundings. Waking up one day and feeling like the world around you is completely off-kilter, yet strangely, nothing externally has changed. It can feel disorienting. I've seen people awaken to their spiritual journey and fall into recluse because they think there must be something wrong with them. They feel changed, see things entirely differently, but no one else does. It can therefore feel easier to turn inward, to isolate themselves. Even though a spiritual journey is personal and intimate, it is not meant to be traveled in a vacuum. To fully embrace your spiritual journey, it requires being out in the world, experiencing life and everything and everyone in it. I wanted to write something that at once felt like a personal spiritual mentor for you as you begin your spiritual journey and give you the confidence to travel it out in the world, connecting with and experiencing life in your new way.

Seeing yourself in a new light can be liberating and coming face-to-face with your blind spots and egoic tendencies can take time to process. I was tired of seeing others hold themselves back because they were overwhelmed with the process, felt alone, or didn't know where to start or go next.

The heaviness of feeling different or alone can give the impression that the spiritual journey is scary and isolating. You may even feel, as I did, like the anomaly in your family, town or city. The reality is that it is the start of a brand new life. When the Seeker within starts speaking to you, and you begin to listen, it is a day of celebration. You are not alone. You never have been. And now you have something along for the ride.

As you live and grow through your personal experiences you'll gain not only the mental understanding of lessons and trials, but you'll begin *feeling* the change happen within you in real time. Days will come when you not only notice a pattern that you've lived out over time, but also see it playing out in the present moment—and can choose differently this time. You'll begin to feel the results of your new choices and over time you'll align with people, behaviours, or values that support you. As your own masks begin to dissolve you'll notice masks on others and you may suddenly find yourself no longer interested in the same events, circles, or activities that you used to. Surrendering to this transformation and flowing with it versus resisting it can bring an ease to your spiritual path.

As you begin to expand your self-awareness, prioritizing your internal world will become the most important aspect of the day. Your spiritual practice and personal rituals will become non-negotiables for you each day. You will spend a lot of time purging the ego's outdated ideas, beliefs, and fears. With each discovery of an old way of thinking or believing, you get an opportunity to replace that mental space with something new, authentic to you, and enriching.

The letting go, and giving freedom to others is one of the most powerful moments in the spiritual journey. When you allow yourself to live your authentic life you naturally emit to others what's possible for them. When you find yourself forcing, chasing, or pleading—remember to check your ego. Send a cease and desist if necessary. The ego craves control, safety, and connection, and will cling to anything or anyone that offers a sense of security—even if it's false.

Please remember to be gentle with yourself along your spiritual journey. The unlearning of habits and thought processes can feel like an exhaustive task, but the brain is capable of changing its ways along with your consistent efforts. You may begin to feel grief at the realization of your patterns and time spent living in old outdated views, and intense emotions around past treatment and situations may take time to transform into impactful, deeply personal, and sacred traits that only you could have. Each person you cross paths with will have a series of events which make them special and whole to themselves, just as your experience is deeply personal to you. If you find yourself comparing, judging or preaching to another on how they should be, please hear me on your shoulder. Your inner compass is between you and the Seeker within, just as another's is within them. When you accept that your North may be someone else's South, you begin to let go of the need to bring people along with you, and grant them the freedom to follow their own inner compass.

It may take time during your "rebuild" to identify or invite a community into your life that aligns with your core values and ambitions. There is no specific speed or pace you need to keep to build connections, but remember that support from others can be extremely beneficial in your journey. Now, it's imperative that you take the time and be intentional about building a strong foundation for yourself and for the life you want to unfold. You do not need to go alone, and there are others on this path who've been through similar experiences. We learn the most by engaging with life and people around us. It's through human connection where we discover within ourselves the spaces and blindspots that require attention.

And yes—there are spiritual thrill seekers out there too. I've witnessed many who feel the need for speed, and will take any upside down thrill loop they can find along the way. They throw themselves into psychedelics, withdraw from society for months at a time, attend extreme retreat after retreat, or rush from one healing modality to the next, all with the intention of the quick bursts of healing, evolution, and expansion. The ride for me is one I want to enjoy. Think river cruise versus skydiving. I've made this clear with myself, my guides, and God. To enjoy the journey towards my final destination is the greatest gift I can give myself, and I'm a sucker for a really good view.

Your guiding tools along the way will be your intuition, the power of your discernment, practicing patience, and being brave in your vulnerability. Take your time to listen to others around you, feeling the words they are saying, and then checking in with your body if it feels right to align with them or not. Cultivating community and trust with others will take as long as it takes, and your spirituality and emotional fitness will be tested during these times of endurance.

There may come a time where you come face-to-face with the truth that some things in your life, no matter how much effort you've put in or how much love you try to infuse, are at an inevitable end. The admission of that can be the most difficult part of the realization, but can result in a powerful moment to embrace your ability to choose and to let go of what is holding you back. Often, we know the areas of our lives that contribute to our unhappiness, but admitting to the source of unhappiness shines a light on the areas of your life that you've tried to keep hidden or ignored. Admitting that you can't fix something—or that it's falling apart—deserves to be met with compassion and care, so that healing within your spirit can begin. When you become intentional and start to recognize aspects of your life that are not serving your highest good, your spiritual practice can help transform the areas that are out of alignment and are creating resistance in your life. Learn to recognize when you begin to feel resistance. The forcing or controlling—subtle or otherwise—will be a clue that resistance has entered the chat and needs your focus.

The things we love and have put in the most effort can be the hardest things to let go. If it's something that is not easy to surrender, but you know it's best for you to do so, please remember to show yourself compassion and grant yourself whatever time you need to honour it and grieve. Just because you've done the best you can, doesn't mean it's best for you. Sometimes life, as hard as our ego tries to control it, is asking us to trust that something greater is working with us. Change doesn't mean we are standing alone in uncertainty, sometimes it's life and the Seeker within showing us what's next.

When we come to these crossroads in our lives, and are wrestling with fear or uncertainty, you can feel an instinctual reaction to run, to turn back. I have done this. I knew the decisions that needed to be made, and I was scared to make them. I knew that the only person that would have the courage to do it would be me, but I still didn't. Not knowing the result was enough to keep me stuck, and freezing myself in limiting relationships and mindsets. My brain twisted itself around beliefs that helped me make sense of my life, ultimately becoming a delusional truth that I clung to. I believed that my unhappiness must be what I was deserving of or the scraps of someone's love was something that I should be grateful for. I truly believed that I was unlovable so anything I was "given" needed to be cherished. I once believed that if I really loved someone, I should give everything I had to them and be okay receiving their bare minimum in return. But selflessness, I've learned, does not always mean self-sacrifice. I felt similarly about work: if I gave everything I have to my job, I believed I would achieve ultimate success. In return, I was being met with "meets expectations" in my performance reviews and removed from key team decisions, as if I was supposed to accept that as a compliment of my efforts. Here's the thing: when we choose fear and stay because we don't know what will happen if we choose differently, the result is more of the same.

The emotional pull that these beliefs and fears have on the psyche and our spirit need to be kept in check. Many of our previous beliefs were created from a hurt or defiant ego, and now that your awareness is online you get to decide if it's ego making the decisions, or you for your highest good. Without your attention the limiting beliefs you have for yourself will run amok, and they will dictate your decision making without you even recognizing it until the damage is already done. In the blink of an eye you can find yourself lost, hopeless, and burnt out with nobody there to assist you but yourself. You are your best support system until you create one around you, and it's time to trust and believe in yourself.

Your spiritual practice is meant to help you better attune to your spiritual, emotional, and physical needs and as a result cultivate a solid base on which you can contemplate the bigger meaning of life and engage with the messages that the Seeker is sending from within. It will remind you to be present to life's experiences and to acknowledge the unrest you feel, as well as integrate the moments of transformation and celebrate overcoming previous limitations. Use your practice to consistently reinforce habits within your life that help you tune into your intuition and inner compass. Over time your relationship with yourself will strengthen and naturally evolve into a harmonic connection between yourself and the Universe around you. The subtle messages will become clearer over time, and the courage to act on inspiration will grow as you develop a deeper trust within yourself.

I came across a quote from Dr. Stone while completing my Polarity studies, and when I read it, I felt the vindication and validation that I had been hoping to hear. "May this work reach the seekers who are looking for a deeper perspective of a common denominator in the healing art. The health and well-being of the people should not be neglected. Without health and happiness, all our modern conveniences are of little comfort to us." I had second-guessed my journey time and time again while growing up, but deep down, I knew that following my truth was my only path forward. This quote solidified my faith in my spirit, and I hope, just as I did, that you receive a sign from the Universe that you are on the right path. Any doubts I had were washed away, and I knew I was exactly where I was supposed to be. My final night in Glastonbury—when my heart burst open at the conference—I was walking back to my flat, reflecting on all the years I felt like an anomaly and how, by following my truth, choosing myself, and assisting others in their healing and energy, everything had come full circle. That evening, and my trip to Glastonbury as a whole, was a testament to not giving up on myself and walking in step with the Universe. I hope that you come to see, as I did, that your differences from others are the very things about you to be proud of—not to be ignored or belittled.

Once and a while you see a sign, read a passage, or hear a saying and it resonates in a way that grabs your attention. You are energy. If something resonates with you it means you are in resonance with it, you've made a deep connection with something, and it's meant for you. These moments are not to be ignored. They have manifested in the Universe specifically for you because you are special. Imagine, in all the Universe and all the billions of people in the world, a sign was generated just for you. Everything from the synchronistic song on the radio, repetitive number sequences, the logo on a business, or the recurring imagery of a destination, are signs not to be missed. With self awareness increasing and your inner world quieting down you'll be able to see and hear these signs more clearly. If you don't feel that you are, just ask for them, and let the Universe surprise you.

From the red brick farmhouse to the heart of Glastonbury, my spiritual journey so far has spanned over twenty years. It has given me hope and carried me through both the most challenging and the most blissful years of my life. Through it all, my spiritual practice has grounded and supported me. Yours will too—if you remain open and curious, honour yourself and your authenticity, and keep moving forward even when it feels impossible. Your greatest life is waiting for you, and inspirations about which direction to take often show themselves when you least expect them, so begin to notice the nudges along the way. They may lead you to a destination you never expected, or to one better than you could ever imagine. I hope you allow yourself to embrace the element of surprise along your journey, trusting that life is calling you forward to something truly special.

The moment you decide to take steps forward in your spiritual journey is the moment you open yourself up to embracing the upcoming challenges in your life—responding to the challenges rather than reacting to them. As you build awareness, strength, and resilience you ensure you are ready for the next phase of your journey. With trust and belief in yourself, you can move from feeling uncertain in the unknown to feeling secure and safe in a moment's notice. Life is so much more than what you learn on the pages of your books; it's also in the experiences we have outside of them. From here on out, engage with life. Take your lessons into unknown territory, learn in the wild, and understand that it's who you are that goes with you everywhere.

You might as well get to know yourself and enjoy your own company. Don't leave parts of you behind at the departure gate because you're afraid to fully commit to life's great adventure. Always remember that you can return to this book as your spiritual companion anytime—for reminders, to refocus, or re-align.

In closing...

May the Seeker within speak loudly;
May you open yourself to listen;
May you discover the freedom to be your truest self;
May you notice the blessings along this ride of life, and;
May you show yourself love and compassion, and find the strength you have within to carry on.

When you feel stuck in your past, remember the possibilities life has available to you, beckoning you to take a step forward. Life is waiting for you to live it, and I can't wait to hear how it unfolds for you. Let your spiritual journey be one of enjoyment—not over-analytical, or loud. I've tried that route for you, so you don't need to. Embrace it, trust it, and love yourself along the way. You're worth it.

From a small town in Ontario, Canada, I wish you happiness and strength. May you find the freedom that comes from listening to the Seeker within, following your authentic path, and opening your heart to life's fullest potential.

Wishing you all the prosperity, courage, and love that this life has to offer. Make sure you go and live it.

With love and in solidarity on the path,
Your fellow Seeker
Stacy Louise Kenney

ACKNOWLEDGEMENTS

I want to start with a heartfelt thanks to my Seeker within who spoke to me loudly and grabbed my attention when it did. It's made life more meaningful and purposeful since I started listening to its guidance, and all the days before I became aware. As I deepen my connection with my Seeker, I walk step-in-step with life feeling more connected to it and all it has available to me.

I want to thank all my fellow seekers that I've met along the way and will meet in the future. Your stories and strength have always reminded me that I'm not alone in this spiritual journey, that I still have some work to do, and the borders that separate our countries do not separate us from our hearts.

I want to thank my family and friends who have known many versions of me and stand alongside me as we navigate this life together. To my parents, who helped bring me into this beautiful life as well as my sister Miranda, who has given me a foundation to expand from and continue to be my greatest teachers and allies. To my nieces Ameliya, Clara, and Lydia and my nephew Jonah: Always remember that Aunt Stacy has your back, and will always be a voice in your corner to live life to the fullest even if your mother raises her eyebrows at us.

And to you, the emerging seekers, thank you for opening your hearts to the words on these pages. May the lessons I've learned act as a gentle guide for you on your spiritual journey.

Special thanks to my editor Michelle, for putting up with endless notes, voice notes, comments, changes and many—so many—questions. We did it! How about another one...? I'm just getting started.

ABOUT THE AUTHOR

Stacy Kenney is a Canadian-born author whose small town roots, fishing derby competitions, love for bonfires, and warm summer nights along the St. Lawrence River has blended itself deep within her soul. With over two decades on her own spiritual path, Stacy brings lived experience, insight, and a lightheartedness to the often unpredictable journey of self-discovery. She is a Polarity Therapy Professional and Registered Polarity Principles Practitioner, recognized by both the American Polarity Therapy Association and the International Polarity Education Alliance.

When she's not guiding others through energetic healing or writing about the spiritual road less traveled, she's likely mapping out a full travel itinerary in under ten minutes (a true superpower), exploring new cultures, or sampling local eats—somewhere between Lake Ontario and a tarmac abroad. You might also find her soaking in the quiet beauty of her garden or stargazing into the night sky—day or night, she tries to stay attuned to the everyday wonders we often overlook.

Though new to publishing, Stacy has been nudged, encouraged, and practically begged to write a book for years. This is her way of finally saying, "Okay, okay—I heard you!" Her hope is that this guide feels like a warm conversation with a friend who's just a few steps ahead on the path. She currently mentors seekers around the globe who have embarked on their spiritual journey and can be contacted through her website www.elevationcoachingglobal.com or on Instagram @thestacykenney

Is It Time to Share Your Story with the World?

If this book sparked something within you—a quiet pull you can't quite name, a persistent tug at your heart, or even a full-blown call to finally tell your story—consider this your invitation.

At **Soul Spark Publishing**, we believe every story matters, and yours deserves to be told with care, clarity, and heart. Whether you're feeling drawn to share your memoir, pass on a legacy, or transform your experiences into powerful, story-driven nonfiction, we're here to guide you.

Our bespoke, high-touch publishing journey ensures your book is crafted with intention, artistry, and emotional resonance. We partner closely with authors who are ready to create something extraordinary: books that echo deeply, linger in hearts, and leave a lasting impact.

If that sounds like you, we'd love to help you begin.

Visit us at **soulsparkpublishing.com**. Your story is waiting.

Other Titles From Soul Spark Publishing

The Me I Didn't See

The 6-Figure Creative: Heal Your Relationship with Money Doing Work You Love

Beautiful Chaos: Embracing the Unexpected

Insights from the Soul: Gentle Conversations With Your Inner Self

Whole Wisdom: Trusting the Connection of Mind and Body

Sacred Fire: Memoir of a Marriage

13 Weeks

www.ingramcontent.com/pod-product-compliance
Lightning Source LLC
Chambersburg PA
CBHW061151120626
46546CB00005B/2019